Russia of the Tsars

PETER WALDRON

HALF TITLE The Romanov double-headed eagle, the symbol of Russian power.
TITLE PAGES St Petersburg and the River Neva during the 18th century.
THIS PAGE The palace at Pavlovsk, built 1780–1825.

First published in
the United Kingdom in
2011 by Thames & Hudson Ltd,
181A High Holborn,
London WC1V 7QX

British Library Cataloguing
in Publication Data
A catalogue record for this book
is available from the British
Library

ISBN 978-0-500-28929-7

Designed by Thomas Keenes
Printed in China through Asia
Pacific Offset Ltd

To find out about all our
publications please visit
www.thamesandhudson.com.
There you can subscribe to our
e-newsletter, browse or download
our current catalogues and buy any
titles that are in print.

Contents

Introduction

The Russian Lands

Tsarist Russia was the largest state in the world, spanning Europe and Asia. The first Romanov Tsar came to the throne in 1613, but the empire rose to the apogee of its power between the accession of Peter the Great in 1682 and the abdication of Nicholas II in 1917. By the end of the 19th century the Tsar's domains stretched from central Europe in the west to the Pacific Ocean in the east, along the entire Asian shore of the Arctic Ocean and deep into the deserts and mountains of Central Asia to the south. The Russian heartland around Moscow was made up of undulating woodland that extended eastwards across most of Siberia. The deep forests that covered much of Russia's Asian lands were wilderness, the domain largely of trappers and explorers. For many Russians, the forest was the epitome of their nationhood, representing their essential connection with the natural world. The critic Ivan Aksakov wrote in 1848, 'It is impossible to convey the impression, the feeling of peace and simplicity…the quiet, the trust and the strength of the Russian countryside…No nature can be as good as ours'.[1]

The south and west of European Russia were dominated by the wide grasslands of the steppe, which opened up into Russia's most productive agricultural areas, the fabled 'black earth' region that produced grain to feed the empire. The flat landscapes that made up a large proportion of Russia's territory were a sharp contrast to the mountainous terrain that lay along much of the periphery. The great barrier of the Caucasus closed the 750 km (466 mile) gap between the Black and Caspian Seas, physically hindering Russian expansion, and

OPPOSITE A detail of *In Countess Mordvinova's Forest, Peterhof*, painted in 1891 by Ivan Shishkin, a member of the Itinerant movement.

The expansive Russian landscape, pictured in Nikifor Krylov's 1827 painting *Winter*.

the mountain peoples of the region offered persistent resistance to the growth of Russian power. In Central Asia, the Russians took control of the mountains of the Tian-Shan and the Altai on the borders of China and Mongolia, while in Russia's Far East, great mountain ranges stretched away east of Lake Baikal, culminating in the volcanoes of the Kamchatka peninsula.

The huge geographical expanse of Russia encompassed great variations in climate. Winter dominated Russian life. Much of the empire experienced very severe winter conditions, with heavy snowfalls and temperatures falling far below freezing. Even in European Russia, the first snow could arrive in November and not thaw until April. Summers were brief and often very hot. These extreme conditions played a crucial role in forming Russia's society and economy. The agricultural growing season was very short, and Russian farmers' prosperity depended on good weather during the concentrated periods of sowing and harvest. The vast distances, exacerbated by the cold snowy winters, made communications difficult. Many of Russia's rivers froze over during the winter months, making water transport impossible. Before the building of the railways in the 19th century, Russians had to take to the roads. This could be a risky business: the writer and doctor Mikhail Bulgakov described the horror of a sleigh journey in winter, 'the rear horse stuck up to its belly in a snowdrift…the horses dragging themselves forward, churning up the snow, the sleigh beginning to rock like a boat at sea'.[2] Travel during the spring thaw could be just as slow and difficult, as Russia's primitive roads deteriorated into a sea of mud.

The population of the Russian state was as diverse as its landscape. By the end of the 19th century, the Russian empire counted more than a hundred different national groups among its 125 million inhabitants. Russians themselves comprised less than 50 per cent of the population of the empire, but together the Slavic peoples (Russians, Ukrainians and Belorussians) made up some 65 per cent. European peoples – with Poles as the largest group – made up a further 15 per cent or so, with the remaining 20 per cent comprising a multitude of small national groups in the Caucasus, Central Asia and the Far East. Only 1.25 million indigenous peoples inhabited the great expanses of Siberia and the Russian north, so

A Central Asian carpet-seller, photographed by Sergei Prokudin-Gorskii around 1910, as part of a project to document the Russian empire.

that despite the huge size of the empire, there were areas of European Russia with significant population pressures.

The diversity of the Russian empire was reflected in its religious and linguistic variety. Russian Orthodoxy was the established church, counting the Tsar among its members. The Orthodox church jealously guarded its privileges, opposing attempts by other religions to gain anything approaching equal status. However, Russia counted substantial numbers of Roman Catholics among its population – especially in Poland – while Islam dominated Central Asia. Eastern religions were found among the peoples of Russia's Far East, while in the Caucasus other forms of Christianity existed alongside Islam. The empire's linguistic diversity was even greater: Russian was the main language of government, but a multitude of Asian languages were spoken in the east, while the Altaic and Uralic ethnic families each included a cluster of different tongues. The Caucasus was home to more than twenty languages, while the European part of the empire included Ukrainians, Poles, Finns and Jews.

The Russian state was unique. Its size and diversity presented immense challenges to its rulers. Though an imperial state, it differed from the other great European empires: Russians never had to venture overseas to acquire their colonies. Instead, Russia spread inexorably out from its European heartland, constructing a state that was indisputably imperial, but was also a single contiguous entity. In order to govern such a state, Russia's rulers learned to wield a power that was unparalleled in Europe. The Tsars argued that their country's uniqueness required a distinctive form of government: the Russian empire could only be controlled if its rulers exercised unlimited authority over the heterogeneous and unruly population. The Tsar was the absolute ruler of the Russian state, ordained to his position by God and not subject to any limitation on his power. Autocracy, the Tsars believed, was essential if Russia were to exist as a single, united state.

Russia's Tsars always emphasized how different Russia was from the rest of Europe. They rejected the tentative steps towards any form of popular participation in government that the other great European states were taking during the 18th and 19th centuries, stressing that Russia came from a different tradition and had no need to follow the European pattern of development. The Russian Tsars were proud

Metropolitan Aleksei of the Orthodox Church (d. 1378) depicted in a traditional stylized 15th-century icon.

of their power and felt no need to apologise for the toughness of their regime. Repression was an essential part of the Tsarist state, as Russia's rulers strove to govern their vast empire with very limited resources. The Tsars fought successive wars to defend and extend their territories: between 1700 and 1917 Russia was never at peace for more than thirty consecutive years. Such a level of military involvement required sustained supplies of both men and money. The Tsarist state had to work hard to man its armies and finance its warfare, and the level of control that this demanded spilled over into every other aspect of government.

The emergence of the Russian state was a slow and uncertain process. The lack of natural frontiers in the forests and grasslands

The Moscow Kremlin's Cathedral of the Dormition (built 1475–79) was the setting for the coronations of the Tsars.

Grand Prince Vladimir I of Kiev, who converted to Christianity in 988, depicted in a 16th-century icon.

that lay between the Baltic and Black Seas made it difficult for cohesive states to emerge; every town that did begin to develop its trading and political power quickly found itself the subject of rivalry from outside. The ebb and flow of peoples across the eastern European plains meant that the Slavic tribes only began to develop any real independence in the 9th century.

Agriculture became an important part of the economic activity of the region and, as farmers settled, less fluid social and political structures became established. The Vikings, the greatest of European adventurers, penetrated deep into the Slavic heartland, intent both on trading and on expanding their political influence. Viking settlements were important in crystallizing the situation, and they were instrumental in creating the first Russian state, Rus, which came into being during the 9th century. Centred on the city of Kiev, the new state faced many challenges, but it was able to expand its influence rapidly in the absence of any serious competing powers. The natural resources of the Russian lands helped to enrich Rus, as its furs, wax and honey were in great demand. Also, more cruelly, Rus had a profitable trade in slaves. This newly emergent power became the centre of attention from its neighbours: ties with the Byzantine state became especially important when the Kievan prince, Vladimir I, converted to Orthodox Christianity in 988. This was a crucial moment in the history of the Russian state, signifying the direction in which Russia was to travel for the next millennium. The adoption of eastern Christianity, rather than Roman Catholicism, set Russia apart from Western European patterns of development. The intellectual tradition that dominated Russian Orthodoxy – and by extension, Russian society – valued mysticism and laid only a limited emphasis on rationality. Orthodoxy remained constant in its ideas and values; it was never riven by a Reformation such as that experienced by Western Christianity in the 16th century. The only significant split in the Russian Orthodox Church occurred in 1666, with a dispute over liturgical issues. The seceding Old Believers continued to argue that they were the true Orthodox, but they always maintained an intense loyalty to the Russian state. Nor was Russia affected by the Renaissance, with its revival of classical ideas and imagery: ancient Greece and Rome held no resonance for Russians.

The newly-Christian Kievan state was not strong enough to

sustain itself for long. Its rulers lost authority and Kiev became fractured by internal dissent as rival princes sought to assert themselves. Civil war broke out and, in these circumstances, the Kievan state was an easy target for incursions from outside. Attacks came from all sides, but most significantly from the south and east. The growing weakness of Kiev was matched by the increasing power of the Mongol empire: its horsemen swept westwards across Central Asia in the 1230s, driving deep into the Russian lands, and in 1240 they took Kiev itself, sacking the city. The Mongol invasion had a profound impact on Russia, isolating it even further from Europe. For more than two centuries the Mongols dominated Russia, extorting financial tribute from Russian princes and imposing their absolute and highly centralized regime. The Mongols had no concern for individual freedom and their conquest of the Russian lands was accomplished with great brutality. They did, however, allow individual princes some power, so long as they continued to pay tribute, and the Grand Prince of Vladimir was permitted to act as the conduit through which tribute was paid to the Mongol Khan.

The Mongol empire was not long able to sustain its grip on power across its huge domains. It soon fractured into separate khanates and the Russians were able to mount challenges against their Mongol masters, culminating in the first Mongol defeat at the battle of Kulikovo in 1380. This victory became established in the Russian consciousness as evidence of their destiny to rule northern Asia. Kulikovo, along with the exploits of Alexander Nevsky (the Novgorod prince who had defeated the Swedes and the Baltic Livonian knights in the 1240s) became part of the pantheon of Russian heroic events. Even though the Mongols recovered from this defeat, it showed that they were not invincible, and the Russian princedoms continued to flex their muscles over the next century.

The process of struggling against Mongol overlordship was instrumental in bringing Moscow to the fore among Russia's patchwork of competing princedoms. Ivan III of Moscow played the central role in extending Muscovite influence in the second half of the 15th century. In 1480 he declared the independence of the Russian lands from Mongol control and, by then, the Mongols were too weak to resist. Ivan III laid the foundations for Russia's emergence by conquering Novgorod, Moscow's chief rival, but the establishment of the

The deeds of Alexander Nevsky (1220–63) were immortalized in Eisenstein's 1938 film, which depicted Russian triumph over a Teutonic enemy.

new Russian state was a slow process. It was another century before Ivan IV – the Terrible – was able to continue Russian expansion by defeating the eastern princedoms of Kazan and Astrakhan, but even he had insufficient strength to protect the Muscovite state against attack from outside. Ivan was overly ambitious, embarking on a war with Livonia in an attempt to expand Moscow's influence in the west, but his fingers were badly burnt: Poland, Lithuania and Sweden put up powerful resistance to Russian expansion. At the same time, Ivan's domains were assailed from the south by the Crimean Tatars, plunging Moscow into crisis. After Ivan's death in 1584, Moscow became severely weakened. Between 1598 and 1613, the Time of Troubles – effectively a period of internecine civil war – almost destroyed the state. Rival nobles fought over the throne and foreign powers took advantage of the situation to extend their reach into the Russian lands. Yet Moscow proved just strong enough to survive and, in 1613, Michael Romanov was elected as Tsar by his fellow nobles, desperate to put an end to the chaos that beset Russia.

Recovery from the stresses of Ivan the Terrible's reign and the Time of Troubles was not easy. The Polish state weakened during the

The reign of Ivan IV, known as 'the Terrible', (1533–84) was marked by increased contact between Moscow and Western Europe, as well as by enormous bloodshed.

IOVAN BASILLI GRĀ DVCA DI MOSCOVIA
stampato nouamente.

17th century, allowing Russia to extend its influence in the south and west. By 1654 Ukraine was incorporated into the Muscovite domains. The emerging Russian state was the product of sustained violence and almost perpetual feuding with its neighbours. The Russian princes had to demonstrate concentrated power as they sought to overcome attacks both from internal rivals and from foreign states. They had to wield absolute power over their subjects in order to mobilize the whole resources of their princedoms in the struggle for dominance. The Moscow princes showed utter ruthlessness: Ivan the Terrible gained his soubriquet from his brutal assassination of men who dared to oppose him, and by his merciless subjugation of his domains. By the mid-17th century most ordinary Russians were serfs, the physical property of their landlords or of the state, unable to move away from their landlord's estates and liable to be punished and returned to their owners if they escaped. The Russian state was very different from its European neighbours. The autocratic rulers of Russia had subjugated both the nobility and the peasantry: the Tsar rode roughshod over all his people.

The election of Michael Romanov as Tsar in the Moscow Kremlin in 1613, which brought the 'Time of Troubles' to a close.

Chapter 1

Peter the Great and the Westernization of Russia

At the beginning of the 18th century, the direction of Russia's development fundamentally changed. After a long period of confused and unstable rule, Russia was transformed into a major European power by Peter I the Great (1682–1725). The start of Peter's reign, however, appeared to presage continued instability: the new Tsar was only nine when he gained the throne in 1682 and the prospect of a regency and continued internecine strife among Russia's nobles loomed. Peter grew up with a keen interest in technology and in the military, and his status as a child ruler allowed him to display an irreverence and disregard for tradition that were to be vital in shaping his reign. He was also a determined and vigorous young man, so that in 1689 when it appeared that his half-sister, the regent Sophia, was seeking to take power for herself, the teenage Peter escaped from her troops and had Sophia locked up in a convent.

In 1694 the twenty-two-year-old Peter took full control of Russia. He was able to lead the Russian army to victory against the Turks at Azov in 1696, and in the following year he went on his first visit to Western Europe. This 'Great Embassy' was one of the formative experiences of Peter's life and it was to have a dramatic influence on the development of Russia itself. The Tsar was exposed to the technological and economic superiority of Western Europe at first hand, and he spent more than a year travelling, spending most of his time in the Dutch Republic and in England. Peter was especially interested in studying shipbuilding, and naval matters were to remain one of his consuming passions throughout his life. He also

Russia's Great Imperial Throne, preserved in St George's Hall of the Winter Palace in St Petersburg.

OPPOSITE Sir Godfrey Kneller's 1698 portrait of Peter the Great aged twenty-six. Naval vessels are visible through the window behind the Tsar.

gained experience of Western technology across a wide variety of areas, including medicine, engraving and optical science. His visit to the West was not just an educational experience, however, since Peter was very conscious of Russia's military position and wanted to use his time abroad to strengthen Russia's relations with other European powers.

When Peter returned to Russia in 1697 he moved quickly to use the experience that he had gained abroad. The Tsar was a man of imposing bearing and quick temper: he was just over 2 m (6 ft 7 in) in height, towering above most of his contemporaries, and while he was modest in his dress and his everyday behaviour, he could also act with great ruthlessness. Peter was determined to transform Russia into a country that could match the Western European powers that he had visited and this required not only economic and political modernization, but also a change in the attitudes of Russians themselves.

After his return from the West, Peter attacked traditional Russian dress and appearance, compelling men to shave off their beards and to wear Western-style dress. While he was successful in persuading most of the Russian nobility to go clean-shaven, Peter recognized that the government could raise money from men who clung on to

The young Russian nobleman no matter how long he has lived abroad and acquired decent and polite manners, once he returns to his fatherland reverts to his former animal existence.

Johann Vockerodt, Prussian diplomat, 1737[1]

their beards and in 1705 he introduced a tax to be paid by bearded men. The aversion to beards among the Russian royal family continued until almost the end of the 19th century: Alexander III (1881–94) was the first emperor to sport a beard since the 17th century.

Such moves were very much secondary to the far-reaching reforms that Peter introduced across almost every aspect of Russian society. The Tsar understood that if Russia was to be able to mount a military challenge in Europe, it needed to develop its industrial base. An army and navy capable of holding their own against Russia's neighbours had to be supplied and maintained. Peter moved quickly to establish ironworks: metal was essential for weapons and eleven factories were constructed within five years. Ammunition works were set up, and a wide range of other industries developed. Peter

Forcing noblemen to cut off their beards was an important symbol of change, as Peter strove to realize his ambition of turning Russia towards the West.

particularly wanted to encourage the manufacture of textiles, rope, leather and glass and the number of factories in Russia grew very significantly during his reign. Industry spread more widely across Russia, with the southern Ural Mountains becoming an important centre for establishing factories. The Russian state played a significant role in the promotion of industry: Russia had a weakly developed economy, dominated by serf agriculture, and it had few resources to invest in industrial development. Russia's farms were not profitable enough to produce sufficient capital to kick start industrial growth, so that the only real source of investment was the government itself. Peter's state not only invested directly in industry, but also dictated what each factory should produce. State involvement in the economy went even further as Peter's government took an active part in regulating trade. The state was granted monopolies on the sale of salt and tobacco, and it had a tight grip on foreign trade, holding a monopoly on the sale abroad of products such as caviar and grain. The state exercised considerable control over Russia's

An 18th-century sign for a ropemaker's guild. The new navy and merchant fleet created a huge demand for rope and other commodities.

trade even where it did not hold a monopoly: Peter's government regulated prices, decided where traders could operate and what they could sell.

This was only part of the apparatus that Peter put in place to increase Russian economic strength (and thereby its military power). Industrial investment and the creation of a powerful army and navy required significantly increased government revenue. Peter changed the taxation system and imposed a poll tax on most of the male population in 1721, which helped to increase the amount of money flowing into the Russian treasury. The poll tax generated more than twice the revenue of the taxes that it replaced. Peter also raised revenue from the peasants who were directly under the control of the state, by making them pay cash to the government instead of working on state lands.

Up to 1700, Russia was governed by a confused and incoherent set of institutions. Peter the Great understood that he needed a more effective system of government if he were to mobilize the resources of his empire. Peter created an entirely new set of institutions that were to act as the foundation for Russian government right up until 1917. He established a Senate, which was responsible for ruling Russia when Peter himself was absent, and nine (later twelve) Colleges that each had responsibility for different functions. Russia was divided into provinces, each with a governor, a regular police force was established and the legal system was reformed.

Peter the Great's Colleges on the banks of the Neva in St Petersburg, in a 19th-century painting of the Russian School. Today the building is part of St Petersburg University.

In 1722 Peter the Great drew up the Table of Ranks, a fourteen-point list of government positions, which showed the equivalence between posts in the military and the civilian bureaucracy. The Table allowed for promotion from the most lowly civilian post – Collegiate Registrar – to Collegiate Assessor, the eighth rank (and a crucial step for a bureaucrat, as its achievement automatically conferred hereditary nobility on the holder). Promotion above that rank took men to the dizzy heights of Privy Councillor, but only the bureaucratic elite could hope to reach the first rank – Actual Privy Councillor, First Class. Nikolai Miliutin, one of the architects of the Great Reforms of the 1860s, began his career in 1838 at the age of twenty as Collegiate Secretary, the tenth rank. By 1844 he had risen to Court Councillor, the seventh point on the table, and eight years later he gained the fourth rank, Actual State Councillor. It then took him a further eight years to rise to the third rank, Privy Councillor, by which time he was already Assistant Minister of Internal Affairs, the summit of his career.

Nikolai Miliutin (1818–72) was one of the enlightened bureaucrats who pushed Russia towards reform in the 1860s.

The great majority of Russia's population were serfs, owned either by noble landlords or by the state itself. The serf population had to be kept under effective control, a task that was beyond the state's direct resources. The army and police force could not hope to exercise authority across the huge, sparsely-populated empire, and so the Russian state needed to have the unquestioning support of its nobility to maintain order. Peter the Great made it compulsory for every nobleman to provide service to the state, either by working in

Tsar Peter sets no store by rich garments, fine furniture, carriages and residences...he gets most satisfaction from contact with simple people. Georg Grund, Danish diplomat, 1710[2]

the government bureaucracy or by serving in the army or navy. He made the prospect more attractive to the aristocrats by instituting the Table of Ranks, which provided a way for nobles to advance to the highest levels. At the same time, the state reinforced its commitment to the system of serfdom, reassuring Russia's nobles that they could continue to enjoy absolute control of the serfs in their ownership. This compact between state and nobility – service in return for serfdom – became the cornerstone of Russia's social structure. Peter the Great created a system that was to endure for more than 150 years and enable the Russian state to turn its attention to its international position, safe in the knowledge that its nobility were keeping the peasant population subdued.

Peter the Great enjoyed military life hugely. As a child he had played at soldiers with his companions and when he took the throne he was determined to transform Russia into a great military power. The development of industry and the guaranteeing of tax revenues formed the foundations on which Russia's army and navy could become fighting forces able to match any Western European power.

An 18th-century Russian grenadier, resplendent in full dress uniform. By 1800, Russia's armies were the equal of any in Europe.

Peter began to expand the army soon after his return from Europe, conscripting peasants as regular soldiers and recruiting both Russians and foreigners into the officer corps. By the end of Peter's reign in 1725 the disorganized Muscovite army had been transformed into an effective fighting force of more than 200,000 men.

Peter's greatest military achievement, however, was the creation of a Russian navy. In his childhood he had become entranced by the sheer pleasure of sailing and by the way in which a ship represented a microcosm of the ideal organized society. During the 1690s, Russian shipbuilding was concentrated in the south as Peter sought to repulse the Turks but, after the victory at Azov, the focus of the Russian navy shifted to the Baltic Sea. A central part of Peter's ambition was to extend Russian power in northern Europe and a major function of the new capital he founded, St Petersburg (see page 28), was to provide a base for Russian power in the region. An Admiralty shipyard was established in the new city in 1705, and its first vessel was launched two years later. In 1718 naval affairs were placed under the control of a separate College in Peter's government, and significant numbers of naval experts were persuaded to come to Russia to guide the construction and development of the new Russian fleet. The regulations that governed the navy drew heavily on Dutch and Danish models, and driven by Peter's personal enthusiasm the navy grew apace. By the end of his reign, the fleet comprised nearly 50 warships

Vedomosti ('News') was the first newspaper published in Russia, and this woodcut of St Petersburg adorned its front page in 1711. Behind the naval vessels, the St Peter and Paul Cathedral is visible.

and more than 80 smaller vessels, manned by a complement of nearly 30,000 officers and men.

Most Russians were illiterate at the beginning of the 18th century, but Peter's ambitions for Russia meant that education had to be improved. He was especially active in establishing a range of professional schools to prepare young men for the armed forces and for Russia's new industries. A Naval Academy was founded in 1715, an Artillery School in 1701 and a School of Mathematics and Navigation in the same year. A foreigner directed each of these institutions and students were sometimes despatched abroad to complete their

studies. Other schools were established in medicine, engineering and mining and their graduates played a crucial role in Peter's modernization of Russia. The Tsar also instituted a system of primary education. Some schools were funded directly by the state but the Orthodox church was also allowed to run its own schools. Although the number of children who attended primary schools during Peter's reign was very small (only a few thousand per year) the foundations of Russian education were laid at this time.

The main thrust of Peter's policies was to transform Russia into a European power. He could only accomplish this by demonstrating Russia's new military prowess and by victory in battle. In 1700 Peter took Russia into the Great Northern War against Sweden, ostensibly on the pretext that the Swedes had slighted him during his journey to Western Europe more than two years previously. Full of bravado, Peter led his troops to besiege the fortress of Narva in October 1700, but he was caught unawares by a rapid Swedish advance. Charles XII comprehensively defeated Peter's army, but the Swedes did not follow up their advantage, allowing Peter to retreat and rebuild his forces. Within two years Russian troops were again moving towards the Baltic coast, and early in 1703 Peter's army took control of the eastern end of the Baltic, almost immediately beginning the construction of the city of St Petersburg. Russia's position remained very uncertain, however: Peter's regime was threatened by rebellions on its eastern and southern borders, and he found himself unable to recruit allies to his campaign against the Swedes. Instead, by 1708 Charles XII planned a major advance into Russian territory with the aim of subduing the upstart Peter. The intervening years had allowed the Tsar to increase the size of his army so that, when Charles launched his advance, more than 45,000 Russian troops awaited a Swedish army numbering less than 30,000. When the Swedes moved to challenge Peter, instead of marching on Moscow or St Petersburg, they marched south into Ukraine, seeing better prospects there for unimpeded progress and hoping to use the region's rich food resources to sustain themselves. The two armies met in June 1709 at Poltava, where Russia inflicted a crushing defeat on Charles XII, forcing the surrender of most of the Swedish army. Charles himself escaped with only a few hundred supporters, and Peter's victory marked Russia's real emergence onto the international stage. As a result of the

OPPOSITE A detail of *The Battle of Poltava*, painted in 1717 by Jean-Marc Nattier for Peter the Great.

St Petersburg

The marshy estuary of the River Neva at the eastern end of the Gulf of Finland was an unpromising site for a city. Nevertheless, Peter the Great's creation quickly became one of Europe's most dramatic urban landscapes. The twin golden spires of the Admiralty and the Peter and Paul Cathedral dominated the skyline, and the city centre was encircled by granite-lined canals. Pushkin wrote of Petersburg's 'austere harmonies',[3] and the dead-straight Nevsky Prospekt (Nevsky Avenue) pierced the heart of the city. The Winter Palace, seasonal residence of the Tsars, was the ceremonial centre of the capital, facing the arc of the General Staff headquarters across the great expanse of Palace Square. St Petersburg was not all grandeur, however: it was a significant industrial centre, and its shipyards, metalworks and chemical and electrical industries employed hundreds of thousands of people by 1900. More than 12,000 men worked at the Putilov metal factory alone. The contrast between privilege and poverty was on show in St Petersburg as nowhere else in Russia.

Jean-Baptiste Le Blond's designs for the new capital city St Petersburg were not adopted, although his focus on the eastern end of Vasilievskii Island did become part of the new city's plan.

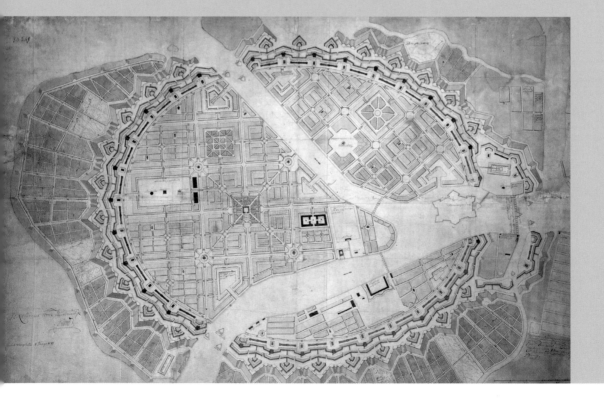

The Menshikov Palace on the banks of the Neva was the most imposing building in St Petersburg when it was constructed in 1710.

Swedish defeat, Russia was able to increase its power in the Baltic, and Russian troops captured the important port city of Riga in July 1710. Peter's overall position still remained far from secure, as the Turks continued to pose a serious threat. A Turkish army was able to inflict a grave defeat on Russia at Prut in 1711, and Peter had to accept the surrender of Azov and surrounding territory to Turkey. The consolidation of Russia's position as a Great Power was a slow process; it was only the signing of the Treaty of Nystad with Sweden in 1721 that finally recognized Russia as a European power to rank alongside Britain, France and Prussia.

Peter the Great's achievement is best symbolized by the foundation of the new capital city of St Petersburg at the empire's northwestern extremity. Peter was determined to make a clear statement that Russia was no longer an inward-looking state, governed from its Moscow fastness, and instead wanted to open a 'window on the west'. St Petersburg was built on European lines, and Peter chose European architects to design a city that showed Russia's new power to the full. The Admiralty and the St Peter and Paul fortress on the banks of the Neva exemplified the power of Peter's Russia and the city quickly became the base for the new Russian navy and a powerful industrial centre. For more than 200 years St Petersburg reminded Russia's rulers of the accomplishments and ambition of Peter the Great.

Chapter 2

Russia's Rural World

Most Russians lived in the countryside and worked as farmers, growing food to feed themselves and their families. When a census was taken in 1719 (in preparation for levying Peter the Great's 1721 poll tax) there were more than 11 million peasants, making up over 90 per cent of the Russian population. Over 175 years later, the 1897 census counted more than 50 million peasants, still comprising 86 per cent of the empire's inhabitants. The peasantry dominated Russia numerically, and the rural world was the key to every element of the empire's life. The government needed peasant men to serve as soldiers and depended upon taxation from the peasantry to finance its wars and other activities; the grain that the peasants grew kept the population fed.

Until the 1860s, most of Russia's peasants were serfs, meaning they were the physical property of either noble landlords or of the state itself. Serfdom had become institutionalized by the mid-17th century as the state sought to tie the peasants to the land to ensure that its nobles had adequate agricultural labour. The serfs had to work on the landlords' estates, labouring in the fields or as domestic servants, or else pay their owners dues in cash or in kind. Some serfs had to do both. The amount of labour and cash that landowners demanded rose gradually but inexorably during the 18th and 19th centuries, as the demand for grain increased and the financial pressures on nobles intensified.

Serfs were forbidden to leave their owners' lands, but this did not prevent some peasants from trying to escape. If they were

Many Russian peasants continued to farm without machinery until well into the 20th century. The scythe and sickle were vital pieces of equipment.

OPPOSITE A peasant family. The samovar and vodka are on the table, and one of the men is playing the balalaika.

Nearly all peasants were serfs before 1861. This 1775 woodcut shows peasants carrying water.

ПОЖ АЛУИ СТА ѾААИ АѦНЕЧІАІЦ НЕСТЫНО ТЕБЕ·
ТЕБЕ ВТО ПОТПЕХИ· АѦНЕ ХУѦЫА СѦЕХИ· ИЗВОЛЬАИШЬ
ЅАѦНОИ БРЕСТИ· АА ГОТОВЗ ВОАУ НЕСТИ· ТОАПОІ ТАНО
ВИ КУВ ЦИ ВПЕ ѦАГОТПОВЬ ГАЕ НАѦЗ АСЛЬ· НЕААРОѦЗ ТЫ
УѦЕНА ПОѦПИВААА· НЕБОСЬ ПТЕПЕРЬ СѦА ВРУЧИН·
ПТЫ ПОПААА·⁘

captured, they could be punished severely and returned to their land-lords. Serfdom was a vital part of the Tsarist regime's armoury in maintaining control over its widely dispersed population. The Romanovs relied on the serf-owning nobility to keep the peasantry subdued: control over the movement of peasants was vital to prevent discontented serfs from staging some form of rebellion against their masters and the Tsarist state. Even serfdom was not a powerful enough deterrent, however: uprisings did take place. For example, in the 1770s a peasant force led by Emilian Pugachev marched north towards Moscow from the Volga provinces, giving Catherine the Great's government real cause for concern before the revolt was put down. By the start of the 19th century, voices were heard calling for the abolition of serfdom, both because it offended against the principles of liberty and rationality that were at the heart of the European Enlightenment and because there was a belief that serfdom restricted the growth of the Russian economy.

Russia's overwhelmingly rural economy made it difficult to stimulate the growth of industry. Russia's farms were inefficient, utilizing strip-farming rather than the larger fields that would have made mechanization feasible. The yields from Russian farms remained consistently below those of Western Europe and the US, making it difficult for Russian landowners to accumulate adequate profits for investment in new industrial enterprises. Serfdom was seen as especially pernicious since it removed all initiative from the peasants, ensuring that they would never seek to improve their land or to increase their output of grain. The moral offence that serfdom represented was magnified by the practical impact that it had on the Russian economy and, by the 1850s, there was a groundswell of opinion among Russia's elites that serfdom must be abolished if Russia was to retain its standing among the civilized nations of the world. The death of the deeply conservative Tsar Nicholas I in 1855 and the accession to the throne of his more liberal son, Alexander II,

Serfs are auctioned, along with a landowner's other possessions, in this 1910 painting by Klavdii Lebedev.

A serf is granted his freedom. Some landowners freed their serfs on moral grounds, but this was rare; serfs were needed to work the land.

provided the opportunity to abolish serfdom. In February 1861, emancipation was proclaimed. The serfs were freed from their land-lords and provided with a plot of land to farm, but the amount of land they gained was usually only just sufficient for their needs, and they also had to pay the government for it. Russian farmers were affronted by this, since they believed that the land they farmed belonged to them by right, and the forty-nine-year period over which they were to make the redemption payments to the govern-ment meant that peasants were permanently reminded of the injustice that they felt had been done to them.

The emancipation of the serfs was the most substantial piece of social change ever implemented by the Tsarist state: it not only liber-ated the peasants, but also brought about fundamental changes for the Russian nobility. In the years after 1861, many Russian nobles decided to reduce their involvement in farming and they sold large quantities of land. The end of serf ownership changed the social balance in the Russian countryside, reducing the power that the nobility could exert over the rural population. Emancipation acceler-ated the process by which the peasant population was becoming more varied: as noble landlords sold land, enterprising peasants were able to buy it to extend their own holdings. The government was keen to encourage this, establishing the Peasant Land Bank in 1883 to offer cheap loans to peasants who wanted to buy more farmland. The abolition of serfdom did allow Russia's economy to develop differently, but the pace of change was very slow. The behaviour of tens of millions of peasant farmers could not be quickly altered, and most

The nearest kerosene lamps are seven miles away at the railway station...the nearest street-lights thirty-two miles away in the district town. Mikhail Bulgakov, writer and doctor, 1916[1]

Russian peasants continued to live in much the same way as they had before 1861.

There were good reasons why the peasantry were so conservative in their behaviour and so reluctant to embrace change. Farming was a precarious business for most Russian peasants: many of them lived on the edge of subsistence, producing just enough to feed their own families. Some parts of the Russian empire – notably the 'black

The wooden plough – the *sokha* – was the central farm implement, light enough to be pulled by a single horse. This photograph was taken in Belarus between 1907 and 1914.

Picking potatoes. Potatoes became an important food source in the 19th century, when potato production increased faster than grain output.

earth' region in the central and Volga provinces – were endowed with rich, fertile soils, but these areas were the exception. Most Russian farmers had to struggle with poor quality, thin soil and the climate made farming even more difficult. Many of Russia's farmers recognized the fragility of their position and tried to diversify their sources of income by working at home during the winter on craft products or, as Russia's factories expanded during the 19th century, by heading to the cities to take up seasonal jobs there. Farming techniques remained largely unchanged: Russia's serfs continued to strip-farm in the traditional way after 1861. Strip farming meant that each

The whole family was needed to work in the fields, especially at harvest and hay-making time when bad weather could ruin a whole year's crops.

farmer in a peasant village could have a share of both the fertile and the less useful agricultural land. Even after emancipation, the communal impulse remained very powerful in Russian villages. In some parts of Russia the strips of land in a village could be redistributed at intervals to ensure that changes in family size were reflected in the share of land that each farmed. Taxes and the redemption payments that were levied after 1861 were collected by village, rather than individually, so that Russia's peasants had a very close degree of interdependence.

Much of the behaviour of Russian peasants was conditioned by the fundamental need to ensure the security of food supply in a very difficult environment. Farmers lived in large extended families, and it was usual for peasants to marry early. Farming families needed to be

A meeting of village elders, who were usually the older and wealthier villagers. The elders dispensed justice and imposed punishments for minor offences.

Peasant Houses

Russian peasant houses were traditionally built of wood, but brick was utilized more during the 19th century. The floor was sometimes made from wooden planks, but was often just hard-packed earth. Straw was plentiful in the countryside and was used to thatch houses and as bedding, as well as for fuel to keep the stove going through the long winter. Heating was of crucial importance and the stove took up much of the living space. Some peasant houses had no chimneys, and visitors often complained about the 'caustic clouds of smoke'[2] that filled rural dwellings. The stove usually had sleeping shelves and in the winter old people spent much of their time keeping warm on the stove. Peasant houses had little furniture, with benches round the sides of the main room that were used both for sitting and sleeping. In the summer, peasants slept in small barns near the house, but in the winter the whole family, along with their domestic animals, had to live in close proximity to each other.

LEFT *Building a timber house.*

BELOW *The sparsely-furnished interior of a peasant house. The samovar is prominent among the family's possessions.*

able to rely on a guaranteed supply of labour and, at a time when infant mortality was high and medical treatment only rudimentary, a large family provided many pairs of hands to work in the fields. Russian farming was a strenuous business and was concentrated into a short period of the year. Spring comes late to Russia and sowing had to be completed quickly to take advantage of the short growing season. Late frosts or early autumn rains could easily destroy a year's

Meat is a great rarity on the peasant table and appears only on great holidays. Fish is eaten even less in places distant from rivers. 1860 report on Riazan province[3]

crops. Harvesting was the climax of the peasants' year and every member of the village community had to play their part in reaping the grain and collecting it before autumn arrived.

Agriculture did not bring great prosperity to most Russian farmers and their lives were simple. Peasants lived in villages, rather than on isolated farmsteads, with their farm animals housed close by so that they could be easily cared for during the long winter months. Good heating was vital for the peasants' homes and a large stove dominated the living quarters, designed to provide constant heat right through the cold winters. Most stoves were wood-fuelled and peasants were jealous of their rights to gather wood from the forests around their village. The peasants' diet was simple, dominated by

FOLLOWING PAGES
A peasant family harvests their crops, in a photograph from the early 20th century. The forest is visible close behind their fields.

Famine struck parts of Russia in 1891, compelling some peasants to rip the thatch from their house roofs to feed their animals.

Peasant women worked as hard as the menfolk, especially during wartime, when men were conscripted in large numbers.

rye bread and vegetables. They ate little meat or fish, and dairy products were also rarely consumed. Even though Russian farmers kept livestock, their animals were too valuable to slaughter for food and the peasants kept them for manure or else to sell. The village drinking house was a central feature of rural village life and drunkenness at holiday times was a regular occurrence.

Most Russian peasants were illiterate. By the 1890s only 20 per cent of the Russian population could read and write, and rural dwellers had lower literacy levels than urban residents. Peasant women in particular had very low levels of literacy, and in some provinces, such as Simbirsk and Penza, fewer than 4 per cent of farming women could read and write. This did not mean that there was no enthusiasm for education. The peasantry recognized that their sons – and, increasingly, their daughters – needed to be able to read and write to engage with the modern world. Still, they took a utilitarian approach to education, placing little importance on the wider cultural benefits that education could bring. Most peasant children received no more than two years of schooling by the beginning of the 20th century and it was very unusual for them to proceed to secondary school.

The peasant world changed only very slowly. This is not surprising, considering that by 1900 there were more than 50 million

Vodka

Vodka played a central role in the life of Russia's peasants. Almost every visitor to the Russian countryside commented on the level of alcohol consumption: the liberal Boris Chicherin bemoaned the 'ruinous drinking' of the peasants and the 'disgraceful commune meetings outside the pub, usually accompanied by three days of drunkenness'.[4] Vodka was an integral part of village celebrations, and heavy drinking was accepted as a vital recreation for the peasant population. The Russian government gained huge revenues from the vodka trade: in 1864 it abolished tax farming for vodka and thirty years later it imposed a full government monopoly on the manufacture and sale of vodka. Almost one third of the Russian state's revenues during the 19th century came from vodka. When, in a fit of patriotic enthusiasm at the beginning of World War I, prohibition was declared, the drastic drop in government tax revenues only added to the regime's woes. Prohibition did not stop the peasantry drinking; they simply switched to home-produced vodka.

The drinking house was a central part of the village scene. This 1889 painting of a tavern is by the Russian artist Timofei Mosgov (1866–1919).

peasants in Russia. After serious peasant revolts during the revolutionary year of 1905, a reforming Prime Minister, Peter Stolypin, attempted to make fundamental changes to the way in which Russian farmers lived. He wanted to move away from the communally-based structures in which agriculture was carried out and to persuade Russia's peasants that they should become independent smallholders on the Western European model. Stolypin believed that this would have significant economic benefits, since it would allow farmers to work on their own initiative, freed from the constraints of the village commune, but he also hoped that it would transform the peasants into conservative small landowners who would have every interest in preserving the political status quo and opposing revolt. This plan was as ambitious as the emancipation of the serfs some forty years before,

Peter Stolypin, Prime Minister from 1906 to 1911. He recognized the need for land reform, but his efforts were frustrated by conservative opposition and the outbreak of war in 1914.

Farmers took every opportunity to maximize their income. These women, photographed between 1907 and 1914, are selling herbs that they have grown.

but it was even more difficult to implement; disentangling the system of strip-farming required careful surveys of village land and much debate to ensure that all the peasants received equally useful parcels of land when they became independent farmers. Stolypin himself declared that Russia needed twenty years of peace for his land reform to become effective. The outbreak of war in 1914 stopped the process in its tracks with less than 20 per cent of Russia's peasants having taken advantage of the new system.

Life was always hard for Russia's farmers. During the 19th century the population of the empire grew inexorably as fewer children died young and life expectancy improved. This placed great stresses on the rural world, as Russian farmers had to produce more grain to feed the ever-increasing number of mouths. By the second half of the 19th century, Russia's population was growing by more than 1.5 per cent annually, expanding from 70 million in 1863 to 175 million by the outbreak of war in 1914. While some of this increase came through the acquisition of new territories, especially in Central Asia, the provinces of European Russia witnessed substantial population growth. Peasant farmers needed more grain to feed their own families, while Russia's expanding cities demanded food for their inhabitants. At the same time, the financial burdens on Russian farmers increased as the government levied higher taxation. Staples of peasant life, such as matches and oil for lamps, were taxed more heavily, while the redemption payments imposed after emancipation also put pressure on the peasant economy. Much of the commentary at the end of the 19th century concentrated on the dismal condition of Russian agriculture and the poverty of the peasantry: Alexander Engelgardt, a Smolensk landowner, wrote in the 1870s that he saw 'decay and destruction everywhere' as he travelled around his district, and he bemoaned the fact that most landowners had sold their estates and that 'many farms were completely neglected'.[5]

It became the accepted view that Russia's villages were poor and that the peasantry were suffering under the twin pressures of ruinous financial exactions and the need to grow more grain. Russia's farmers behaved rationally enough in the face of threats to their existence: many decided not to pay the redemption payments that they owed. Less than twenty years after emancipation, arrears had reached more than 20 per cent of the amount due. By 1905 the level of arrears was so high that the government cancelled all outstanding redemption payments. For the farmers, paying off the government was an unproductive use of their cash, and anyway they resented the imposition of these levies. Peasants instead used their resources to enhance

This 1906 photograph shows two rural policemen with a farmer, in the area of Lebediansk. Rural police and troops often used great violence to control the peasantry.

their economic position: they bought up or rented land from landowners who were divesting themselves of their estates. In this way, Russia's farmers were able to expand their production to cope with the rising population and grain output grew faster than the population increased. Russia was able to export grain at the end of the 19th century.

The Russian countryside always dominated the landscape of the empire. Farming determined the prosperity of Russia and the attitude of the peasantry had a crucial impact on the economic and political development of the country. When the Tsarist regime collapsed in the winter of 1917, there was no groundswell of popular enthusiasm in the countryside for Tsar Nicholas II. The monarchy had failed to persuade the farming population that the continuation of Tsarism was in their interests and the peasantry sat by indifferently as Nicholas II and his regime were pushed out of power.

Isaac Levitan's 1895 painting *Golden Autumn*, with its birch trees and slow-moving river, captures the mood of Russia's northern landscape.

La Situation de La Pologne en MDCCLXXIII.

Die Lage des Königreichs Pohlen im Iahr 1773.

Chapter 3

The Tsars Triumphant, 1750–1850

Peter the Great's demonstration of Russian power in Europe was only the beginning of a process of sustained Russian expansion. By the time of Peter's death in 1725, Russia was established as a northern European power of considerable authority, and had supplanted Sweden as the dominant state in the eastern Baltic. Yet this was only the start of the transformation of Russia into a great imperial state, dominating the Eurasian land mass. During the 18th century, Russia asserted its position in Europe, gaining control of much of Poland. Both Russia and Frederick II's Prussia had designs upon the weak Polish state, seeing it as ripe for dismemberment. In 1772 the first partition of Poland gave Russia, Prussia and Austria slices of Polish territory, leaving a much weakened Polish state centred on Warsaw. This did not satisfy the ambitions of the three powers, however, and in the 1790s the Polish state was again their target. In 1793, Russia and Prussia seized more Polish territory, and two years later Austria joined in the final partition of the country, wiping independent Poland from the map of Europe. Russia had gained the majority of Polish territory, and this sharpened Russia's appetite for further expansion.

After 1800, however, Russia was faced with the growing Napoleonic empire. Tsar Alexander I (1801–25) met Napoleon at Tilsit in 1807 and the two emperors signed an alliance, but this offered Russia only a short respite from the wars that were engulfing Europe in the wake of the French Revolution. In 1812, Napoleon's Grande Armée marched eastwards, crossing the River Niemen into Russia in April and marching towards Moscow. By early September,

OPPOSITE A cartoon showing Catherine the Great dividing up Poland in 1772 with Joseph II of Austria and the Prussian king Frederick the Great.

BELOW Tsar Alexander I met Napoleon Bonaparte at Tilsit in 1807. The meeting took place on a raft moored in the River Niemen, as depicted in this 19th-century print.

Napoleon was only 120 km (75 miles) from Moscow and the Russian army decided to make a stand against the French at Borodino. The battle was extremely bloody, and 70,000 soldiers were killed or wounded, but the Russians proved unable to halt the French advance and Napoleon entered Moscow a week later. This apparent disaster proved to be only a temporary setback for Russia, however, as the French soon began to retreat. In the winter of 1812 they were driven out of Russia by Alexander I's armies. Allied with Prussia and Austria, Russia was instrumental in the defeat of Napoleon and in March 1814 Tsar Alexander I led his troops down the Champs-Elysées in Paris.

Russia was able to take advantage of the confused situation in Europe by adding Finland to its domains in 1809 after a short war with Sweden, so that by 1815, the Russian empire was firmly established as one of Europe's most powerful states. The victory over Napoleon was of immense significance for Russia. It demonstrated that, in little more than a century, the Romanov state had developed from a merely regional power to one that could not only withstand an assault from the greatest European land power of the time, but also turn the tables on it, crushing France and bringing an end to Napoleon's empire. The symbolism of the Russian victory played a vital part in the construction of the idea of the Russian nation during

Napoleon is caricatured in this Russian depiction of his retreat from Moscow in 1812. His ignominious return to France is a far cry from his triumphant march eastwards earlier in the same year.

Portrait by Mikhail Ivanovich Terebenev of Field Marshall Kutuzov (1745–1813), whose cautious approach to confronting Napoleon was vindicated by the eventual Russian victory. Kutuzov died before the final defeat of the French.

the 19th century: Tolstoy's great novel *War and Peace* attributed the Russian triumph to the resilience and innate good sense of the peasantry that made up the army. The aged Field Marshal Kutuzov, who commanded the Russian troops at Borodino and then allowed Napoleon to occupy Moscow, was portrayed as the archetypal peasant, wise and resistant to the more flamboyant western elite of the Russian army who argued for a much more assertive approach to the French. The war of 1812 was christened the 'Patriotic War' and, even at times of military setbacks for Russia, it remained a potent symbol of Russian glory. In 1912 the centenary of Napoleon's defeat was celebrated with a visit from Tsar Nicholas II to the battlefield at Borodino, and the event was portrayed as commemorating a time when the Russian people were united in defence of their homeland.

Russia's army was a formidable force by 1815. The army and navy consumed the majority of the state's budget and the Russian military was the largest of the European armed forces. Catherine the

Portrait of Paul I (1796–1801) by Borovikovsky, 1800. Paul was a martinet who blamed his mother, Catherine the Great, for the assassination of his father. At her funeral, he ordered that his father's remains be disinterred and carried to the grave alongside hers.

OPPOSITE Egor Botman's 1849 picture of Nicholas I portrayed him more sympathetically than the military poses in which the Tsar was usually depicted.

Great's son, Tsar Paul I (1796–1801) was deeply interested in the army and gave the Russian state a much more overtly military outlook. Even after Paul's assassination, this focus on the army continued until the end of the Romanov regime. Each of the 19th-century Tsars paid great attention to their army, very conscious that their regime depended on military power for its survival. Tsar Nicholas I (1825–55), whose accession to the throne had taken place during the Decembrist revolt – an attempted military coup – was unbending in his determination to use the Russian army to put down rebellion wherever it occurred. A popular uprising in Poland in 1830 was quashed (with great force) by Russian troops, and the Tsar gained the soubriquet of the 'gendarme of Europe'[1] for his tough and unrelenting approach to dealing with dissent.

The Romanovs became very confident about their power and position during the first part of the 19th century. They had vanquished enemies at home and abroad and their empire was spreading rapidly into Asia and the Caucasus. During the 1830s, the imperial Russian state developed what amounted to an ideological justification of its position, emphasizing the importance of the autocratic monarchy for Russia and stressing that the huge expanse of the empire and its diversity of peoples and landscape made absolute rule essential for the continued unity of the state. Still, political power alone was not enough to maintain the power of the Romanovs: the Russian empire was enormous and the state had only a relatively small number of bureaucrats to govern it. The Tsars enlisted the Russian Orthodox church to support the Tsarist regime. Peter the Great abolished the patriarchate – the clerical head of the church – in 1700, subordinating the Orthodox church entirely to the state and installing a bureaucrat to head the church as Procurator of the Holy Synod. Orthodoxy became an important buttress for the Tsarist state, as bishops and local priests preached that the Russian people had a duty of obedience to the Tsar and that rebellion was not only unlawful, but also sinful. The state gained an important means of communicating with its subjects through the parish priests: the

One could not be more emperor than Nicholas I...his voice is unforgettable, so full of authority it is, so solemn and firm...this voice belongs to a man born to command.

Marquis de Custine, French aristocrat and travel writer, 1839[2]

ABOVE LEFT Russian Orthodox clergy were usually among the few who could read and write. Often poor, they were an integral part of the rural community.

ABOVE RIGHT Ilya Repin's *Religious Procession in the Province of Kursk* (1880–83) shows every aspect of Russian provincial life, from devout peasants to the haughty local policeman on horseback.

manifesto announcing the emancipation of the serfs in 1861 was written by a bishop and was first read from the pulpit in Orthodox churches. The Orthodox church itself gained a hugely privileged position in Russian society. Other religions had a much inferior status; it was difficult for them to construct churches or to recruit new converts to their religion. Church and state worked very closely together, understanding that it was in both their interests to support one another. Autocracy and Orthodoxy presented a formidable combination in maintaining the established order, and they were complemented by official promotion of 'Russianness' among the varied national groups that comprised the empire. The St Petersburg regime ruthlessly tried to make its empire uniformly Russian, with the Russian language taking priority and indigenous peoples subordinate to their Russian masters.

International prestige also helped to bolster the position of Russia's rulers at home. Nevertheless, the Tsars faced considerable challenges and they could never rest on the laurels that their foreign victories brought. Russia's political and social structure was far from stable enough to prevent the emergence of dangerous threats to authority, and it was a risky matter to become a Russian Tsar. Peter III, Paul I and Alexander II were each assassinated, and both Catherine the Great and Nicholas I faced rebellions that came close to toppling them. The last Tsar, Nicholas II, was murdered along with his family in July 1918, bringing the Romanov dynasty to an end in a

Tsarskoe Selo

In 1717 Peter the Great began to build a new imperial residence just south of his capital city of St Petersburg, naming it the Catherine Palace in honour of his wife. The vast palace – its façade eventually stretched for more than 300 m (984 ft) – was subsequently hugely embellished by Catherine the Great. It was the centrepiece of the imperial domain of Tsarskoe Selo, literally 'Tsar's Village', which became the main country residence of Russia's rulers. The opulence of the Catherine Palace, with its startling blue façade and the glistening gold of its chapel's onion domes, was reflected in the exuberant towers and pavilions scattered across the huge park that surrounded it. However, for most of the 19th century the Tsars preferred to live in the less ostentatious and more homely Alexander Palace close by. Catherine the Great had built this palace for her grandson, the future Alexander I, and it was there that the last Tsar Nicholas II and his family made their home, living the life of country gentry, away from the bustle and dangers of St Petersburg itself.

The Arabesque Hall in the Catherine Palace was designed by Charles Cameron in the 1780s.

cataclysm of violence. The threats faced by Russia's Tsars encouraged them to extend their power as much as they could and to present an image of untrammelled authority both to their own subjects and to the world outside Russia. Buildings were an important part of the image of grandeur that the Tsars wished to create. St Petersburg itself was founded in 1703 by Peter the Great to demonstrate the power of the expanding Russian state, and over the following century the Tsars and their relatives constructed a series of great palaces in the

The palace at Gatchina was a favourite of both Paul I and Alexander III, and its courtyard was the venue for military parades.

countryside around the city. Catherine the Great (1762–96) was responsible for the most splendid of these palaces at Tsarskoe Selo (see page 55), the opulence of which proclaimed the wealth and power of the Russian monarchy. At Gatchina, Oranienbaum, Peterhof and Pavlovsk more huge palaces were built, solid demonstrations of the wealth and power of the Romanovs.

The Romanovs' dominance came at a price, however. The Russian peasantry posed a continuing threat to the regime and the system of serfdom, which persisted until the 1860s, gave Russia's rulers constant worries. The development of Enlightenment thought during the 18th century, with its emphasis on the importance of human rights and individual liberty, put pressure on Russia's rulers to abolish serfdom and give the peasantry their freedom. Catherine the Great was especially keen to portray herself as in tune with the great thinkers of her time, and she corresponded with Voltaire and Diderot, but she drew the line at putting any of their ideas into practice. Russia was too different from Western Europe for the Enlightenment to be relevant, Catherine argued, and she continued to insist that serfdom had to continue in Russia if the state were to maintain control of its subjects.

The regime's need to exercise authority over the peasantry continued to be a paramount concern during the first half of the 19th century. Tsar Nicholas I was deeply reluctant to countenance real agrarian reform, preferring to maintain the peasantry in a state of servility. Such attitudes had been formed by the experiences of peasant rebellion during the 17th and 18th centuries. Revolt had swept through the Russian countryside in 1606–07 and again at the

Stepan (Stenka) Razin stirred up widespread peasant unrest in 1670 by promising to destroy noble power. Captured by Muscovite forces in 1671, he was brutally executed.

beginning of the 1670s, when Stepan Razin's Cossack horde advanced up the Volga. Forty years later, Bulavin led an inchoate mass of peasants in rebellion against Peter the Great's regime. Each time, the Russian government mobilized its army to put down the rebellions and the uprisings failed, but they were a constant reminder of the potential danger from the tens of millions of peasants. By far the most serious threat to the Russian Tsars came in the 1770s when the Cossack Emilian Pugachev proclaimed himself to be the deposed

The young Catherine the Great, painted by Vigilius Eriksen (1762–64). Her imperious profile suggests the determination that would characterize her thirty four years on the Russian throne.

For nearly twenty years during the reign of Catherine the Great, Grigory Potemkin occupied a place at the centre of the empress's affections and the empire's politics. He was first introduced to Catherine in 1774 and they rapidly became lovers; it is possible that the two were secretly married at some point. Catherine placed great trust in Potemkin and, even though he was supplanted in her bed by a series of other men, the empress gave him a series of crucial military commands. He was despatched to southern Russia to quell rebellion in the Crimea and his success was rewarded with the governor-generalship of the region. He led Russian troops to victory over the Turks in 1788, but died suddenly in 1791. Catherine was grief-stricken. She wrote:

You have no idea of my state of affliction...we understood each other perfectly. I regard him as a very great man, who did not fulfil half of what was in his grasp.[3]

Potemkin, shown here in a portrait by an anonymous painter, rose from humble beginnings to the highest levels of the Russian state. He was awarded the title of Prince by Catherine for his subjugation of the Crimea.

After the defeat of the rebel Emilian Pugachev, he was brought to Moscow in an iron cage. Catherine the Great ordered that he must not be tortured and he was executed in January 1775.

Tsar Peter III and gathered a peasant army that took control of much of Russia between the Volga and the Urals. Catherine the Great turned the state armies on Pugachev: he was defeated and his revolt put down with great force. Never again did the Russian peasantry seriously endanger the survival of the regime. The absolute power of the state and the ruthlessness of Russia's rulers had proved equal to the task of subduing revolts.

The Romanov regime based its power on conscripting a formidable army and on ruthlessly collecting the taxes needed to maintain it. By the mid-19th century, Russia's army was more than twice the size of its nearest rival, France, and Russia was able to recover from

Any serfs and peasants who cease to give proper obedience to their landlords shall be punished by the knout and forthwith deported to Nerchinsk for penal servitude for life. Decree on serfs, 1767[4]

the immense costs of losing the Crimean War (1853–56). The huge strength of the Russian state meant that it was able to resist calls for reform until the first years of the 20th century. Successive Tsars toyed with the idea of engaging the wider population in the work of government in some form, but until the 1860s none was prepared to take any action that would limit the autocratic power of the sovereign. Catherine the Great was prepared to debate the theory of representative government, but not to put those ideas into practice. Her son,

Paul I, tried to increase the power of the state, stressing the role of the military and imposing substantial regimentation on the Russian nobility. Even the Romanov regime, however, was not powerful enough to dictate to its social elites how they should work, and Paul's martinet-like behaviour antagonized the nobility. After he had ruled for less than five years, a group of nobles decided to force the emperor to abdicate. They confronted him in his bedroom one night in March 1801 and in the ensuing melée Paul was strangled to death.

Paul's son, Alexander I, appeared to set a new, more liberal tone and he was pressed by his advisers, led by Michael Speransky, to make reforms. But Alexander, too, resisted the pressure for change. Russia's military victory over Napoleon helped persuade him that the Russian state was in good shape and that there was no need for reform. For the last decade of his reign, Alexander I pursued a traditional set of policies, establishing military colonies in the countryside to develop Russian agriculture and to display the authority of the state to the peasantry. On Alexander's death in 1825, reform-minded army officers attempted to deny the throne to his chosen successor Nicholas I in favour of his older brother Constantine, believing he would be more likely to undertake reforms. On a freezing December day, the rebels assembled 3,000 troops on Senate Square in the heart of St Petersburg, hoping to prevent Nicholas from taking power. Showing the ruthlessness that was to be the hallmark of his thirty years on the throne, Nicholas faced down the Decembrist revolt and by nightfall the rebels had been defeated. The government condemned its five leaders to be publicly hanged and sentenced hundreds of their followers to exile in Siberia. For the next three decades Nicholas ruled Russia with great firmness, determined to prevent any repetition of the rebellion that had threatened his accession.

When revolutions broke out across Europe in 1848, Russia remained aloof from the ferment that was gripping much of the continent. During the 1820s and 1830s Nicholas I had stamped firmly on even the slightest expression of dissent, establishing a secret police – the Third Section – in 1826 and going so far as to censor personally the works of prominent authors. Alexander Pushkin, Russia's greatest poet and an associate of some of the Decembrist rebels, had to submit his work for the Tsar to approve before it was published. The firm stance adopted by Nicholas was successful in stemming the

The radical critic, Alexander Herzen, placed the five executed Decembrist leaders on the cover of his underground journal *Poliarnaia Zvezda* ('Polar Star') in 1855.

growth of overt discontent, but this came at a price. The frozen society that he created could not be sustained and, by the 1840s, many of Russia's social elite knew that change was on the horizon. The 'enlightened bureaucrats'[5] who were in the ascendancy by the middle of the century believed that Russian strength – both at home and abroad – would allow them to reform Russia successfully, but the events of the 1850s were to demonstrate the fragility of the Tsarist regime's grip on power.

Alexander I (1801–25) is shown as a great military leader in this 1837 portrait by Franz Krüger. The picture was immediately hung in the War Gallery of 1812 in the Winter Palace.

КАРТА АЗІЯТСКОЙ РОССІИ

СОСТАВЛЕНА ПО НОВѢЙШИМЪ СВѢДѢНІЯМЪ

ГЕНЕРАЛЬНАГО ШТАБА

ПОЛКОВНИКОМЪ ИЛЬИНЫМЪ.

МАСШТАБЪ въ Англійскомъ дюймѣ 250 верстъ

Chapter 4

Building an Empire

Tsarist Russia was both a European power and a great imperial state. Unlike the empires of the British, French, Spanish and Dutch, with their far-off overseas colonies, the Russian empire was a united state within a single border. Russian imperial expansion was an inexorable process as Russians moved east and south away from the forested Muscovite heartland. There were few natural frontiers to obstruct Russian progress in western Asia and the Russians could expand easily, hindered only by the climate they encountered as they moved further east and south. Explorers and horsemen ranged swiftly across the grasslands of western Siberia, allowing Russia to establish trading bases and military outposts. The plains of Central Asia, over which Genghis Khan's Mongols had swept unhindered on their way to conquer the Muscovite state in the 13th century, offered few obstacles to Russian troops 600 years later, as the Tsarist empire expanded. It was only in the Caucasus and in parts of Central Asia that the Tsarist regime encountered real opposition to its imperial expansion, and it was able to acquire Siberia and the Pacific Far East almost unchallenged. The Russians also found it easy to acquire new territories in Asia, since the influence and power of China – the most substantial Asian state – was gradually waning and it put up little real resistance. Much of northern Asia was very sparsely populated, offering limited resistance to the Russian advance, and during the 18th and 19th centuries the Russian state was sufficiently powerful and assertive to seize control of these vast lands. International political rivalry also drove the Russians to expand their territories. The St

Geographic information cards, such as this one about Cherkassk, the centre of the Don Cossack region, helped teach Russians about their growing empire.

OPPOSITE Russia was quick to map its new possessions: this 1868 map shows the Urals and Western Siberia.

Petersburg regime was continually concerned that, if it did not take control of these Asian lands, then other European powers would begin to encroach and pose a substantial threat. In the 1850s, Russia became especially concerned about European activity along the Pacific coast and it began to take steps to strengthen its position in the Far East. During the following decade, the Tsar's troops moved into Central Asia, seizing control of the khanates of Khiva and Bukhara, and this expansion was seized upon by the British as proof of Russian intentions to threaten their Indian empire. British moves to strengthen their defences along the northwest frontier of India

Russia's expansion is not an invasion, not a movement of peoples, not colonial, but a distinctive world, moving in all directions and occupying its own land.

Alexander Herzen, radical writer and thinker, 1857[1]

were, in turn, seen by the Russians as evidence of British designs on Russian Central Asia. The intensified rivalry between the two great imperial states drove the Russians on to consolidate their hold on Central Asia and to expand their domains as far as their resources allowed.

Empire also brought wealth. The inhospitable Siberian lands contained rich reserves of minerals and the fur-bearing animals that roamed the cold forests were much in demand by trappers. There was a near-inexhaustible supply of timber: wood became one of Russia's chief exports. Commerce stimulated the development of communications across Russia's vast territories and it also acted as a stimulus for Russians to migrate from the crowded agricultural lands of European Russia to the distant areas that came under St Petersburg's control during the 18th and 19th centuries. Still, migration to the far-flung reaches of the empire was a challenging enterprise, involving months of travelling with no guarantee of a better life when the migrants finally reached their destination.

The Caucasus, the range of high mountains between the Black and Caspian Seas, was the first area into which Russia tried to expand its power. The Tsars naturally wished to control the mountains that formed a natural frontier with Persia and Turkey to the south, and Peter the Great launched an expedition to the Caspian Sea in 1722, intending to prevent expansion northwards by the Turkish Ottoman

empire. However, the Caucasus was populated by proudly independent peoples and the mountains, cut by deep valleys, made it very difficult for troops to establish control of the region. The gradual weakening of the Turkish empire made it easier for Russia to flex its muscles in the Caucasus, and in the first half of the 19th century Russia fought a series of wars that ended with St Petersburg consolidating its dominance in the region. Although these conflicts were violent and bloody, the Caucasus gained a deeply romantic image among Russians. Poems by Pushkin and Lermontov gave an idealized picture of the beauty and wildness of the Caucasus, and this

The Caucasus proved a hard nut for the Russians to crack. This painting by Grigory Gagarin depicts a battle between Russian troops and Circassians near Achatl in 1841.

A couple in traditional dress posed for a portrait in the mountainous interior region of Gunib on the north slope of the Caucasus Mountains, in what is today the Dagestan Republic of the Russian Federation.

encouraged young men to serve in the army there. Leo Tolstoy travelled through the mountains with his brother in the early 1850s, drawing inspiration from the landscape and beginning his serious literary work while he was in the region. The Caucasus became a source of fascination to Russians: the Imperial Geographical Society established a branch there in 1851 and, despite the danger from rebels in the region who continued to oppose Russian rule, Tsar Alexander II journeyed to Dagestan in 1871, protected by formidable Cossack bodyguards. By the end of the 19th century, the Caucasus was becoming a destination for visitors, and mountaineers were making ascents of the great peaks that rose to heights of more than 5,000 m (16,400 ft). The exotic scenery, together with the food and wine, the ancient culture and the variety of its peoples and languages continued to ensure that the Caucasus exerted a powerful attraction for Russians, even though the region remained dangerous and politically unstable. The young Stalin, a native of the Georgian mountains, carried out a series of daring bank robberies in Tiflis (modern Tbilisi) and Baku in the early years of the 20th century, reinforcing the image of the Caucasus as wild and untamed.

It was the great expanses of Siberia, however, that were the central attraction for Russian explorers and colonists. Siberia came to occupy an almost mythical status in Russian thinking, its extremes of climate and landscape offering Russians the opportunity to explore vast wildernesses of forest, cut by great slow-moving rivers. Lake

After Bering's voyages, the Russian Academy of Sciences published this 1775 map showing the areas he had explored along Russia's Pacific coast.

Exile

In 1876 the sixteen-year-old Sergei Shvetsov was sentenced to hard labour for his part in a group that was spreading revolutionary propaganda in Novgorod. His youth meant that his sentence was commuted to exile in Siberia and he spent eighteen years banished to the Surgut region, 2,000 km (over 1,200 miles) northeast of Moscow. He wrote of the 'wild, almost unpopulated landscape...where winter began at the end of September and ended only in May'.[2] Siberia was used as an open-air prison by the Tsarist authorities, but life there was not always difficult. In 1839 the young Alexander Herzen was exiled to the northern province of Viatka, where his university education persuaded the provincial governor to employ him in his chancellery, collating statistical information to be sent to St Petersburg. In some places, however, local officials imposed severe punishments on political prisoners, forbidding them to send or receive letters and placing them under close police surveillance.

Prisoners being hustled along by Tsarist policemen on the way to exile in Siberia.

Inmates in the Alexandrovskii prison in Nerchinsk, 645 km (401 miles) east of Lake Baikal in Siberia. Political prisoners were sentenced to hard labour here.

The sheer remoteness of the Siberian prisons made escape difficult, but the Tsarist authorities could chain prisoners as punishment.

Baikal, the largest freshwater expanse of water in the world, gave way to mountain ranges stretching eastwards to the Pacific Ocean, with the volcanic Kamchatka peninsula extending south. In 1741, Vitus Bering led a Russian naval expedition that landed on the Alaskan coast and this Great Northern Expedition provided the first charts of the Russian Pacific coast. Exploration stimulated the development of the fur trade, and the prospect of great wealth persuaded others to venture east. Siberia also gave young Russians a sense of freedom: far away from the increasingly restrictive atmosphere of St Petersburg, they felt that they could express their own opinions without fear of retribution from officialdom. More ominously, the remoteness of Siberia (before the construction of the Trans-Siberian railway at the end of the 19th century, it took a month to travel from St Petersburg to Irkutsk) meant that the Tsarist regime used it as a prison for its political opponents. Thousands of prisoners were forced to embark on the long and arduous journey into the Siberian forests, but when they arrived, their lives as exiles were often far from disagreeable. Siberian exiles could live in relative freedom, able to receive books and to write. Most of the Bolsheviks who went on to make the revolution of October 1917 had spent time exiled in Siberia.

Migration to Siberia was a difficult undertaking for Russian peasants. More than a quarter of migrants returned to their original homes.

Military priorities played a vital part in the Russian imperative to explore and colonize Siberia and the Far East. The waning Chinese state still posed potential difficulties and there was great pressure from the Russian General Staff to increase the pace of migration to the sparsely-populated eastern lands and to construct a railway to the Pacific. The construction of the Trans-Siberian railway took nearly twenty years; the final tracks were laid only in 1912. The railway helped to encourage Russian peasants to move eastwards, but the government still had to offer substantial financial inducements to migrants to persuade them to make the leap into the unknown that the long journey to Siberia represented.

Central Asia was the final area that Russia colonized. As in the Caucasus, military force played a decisive part in the extension of Russian power: at the end of the 1850s Russian military detachments were sent to take control of part of Kyrgyz territory, but the main phase of the Russian conquest of Central Asia began in 1864. In June 1865, Tashkent fell and this was the beginning of Russia's final victory over the Asian khanates. The army of the emir of Bukhara was destroyed in battle in May 1866. The emir bowed to the inevitable and formally accepted Russian domination. Russian troops then turned their attention to the Khiva khanate: this proved to be a harder nut to crack and it was only in 1873 that the khanate became a Russian protectorate. By the end of the 1870s most of Central Asia lay under

OPPOSITE Driving the Trans-Siberian railway through the wild Siberian landscape. More than 70,000 labourers worked on the railway, cutting down 108,000 acres of forest.

Russian control. The population of Russian Central Asia had reached 7.5 million by the beginning of the 20th century, and this substantial Muslim population presented the imperial authorities with considerable problems. Initially, the Central Asian population had been exempted from military service, but in mid-1916 the government decided to conscript 480,000 of the local male population to work on the construction of military fortifications. This provoked a vast and bloody uprising in which tens of thousands were killed, and which was only put down at the cost of thousands of Russian troops' lives.

Our military conquests in Asia bring glory not only to Russia; they are also victories for the good of mankind. Carbine bullets and rifled cannon bear...elements of civilization.

Nikolai Przhevalskii, army officer and explorer, 1877[3]

By the end of the 19th century, the Russian empire included more than one hundred different ethnic groups, ranging from 55 million Russians to the few thousand Izhora in northern Russia. The Slavonic languages of European Russia gave way to the Uralic tongues of the north and the Altaic tongues of Central Asia. The 1.3 million people of the Caucasus spoke more than a dozen languages between them, and in the Far East, the empire was populated by peoples speaking Mongol and Manchurian languages. This linguistic diversity was reflected in the religions that were practised across the empire: the Russian Orthodox church held sway in most of Russia, but in Poland the Roman Catholic church dominated the scene and most of the Finnish population were Lutheran. Away from European Russia, the religious situation became extremely complex with a large Muslim population in Central Asia and eastern religions in the Russian Far East. The Russian empire encompassed the most varied population of any single state on the globe and its multi-ethnic nature presented immense challenges for the government. The capital city, St Petersburg, was located at the far northwestern corner of the empire and communications with the distant extremities of Russia's domains took many weeks. The peoples that Russia had gathered under its tutelage were frequently unhappy about Russian imperial domination and the Tsarist regime was continually confronted with rebellions and challenges to its authority. The Poles rose in revolt in

Nikolai Przhevalskii

The buccaneering Nikolai Przhevalskii was one of 19th-century Russia's greatest explorers. An army officer, he led his first expedition to the Ussuri region of the Russian Far East in 1867 at the age of twenty-eight, spending two years exploring the frontier with China. In the 1870s he travelled into Central Asia, journeying through Mongolia and Tibet. Lhasa eluded him, but in the course of five long expeditions he travelled more than 30,000 km (18,640 miles). Przhevalskii, however, was not just an explorer: he wanted to promote Russian imperial expansion. 'Scientific research,' he wrote, 'will camouflage the political goals of our expedition'.[4] In 1884 he composed a memorandum entitled *New Thoughts on War with China* for the Russian War Ministry, hoping to persuade the government to launch an attack that would take Russian troops to Peking, arguing that Russia was inherently superior to China and that victory would be an easy matter. The Russian government rejected his ideas, but were happy to continue to fund his imperialist expeditions.

Przhevalskii projected the image of a buccaneer, enduring great hardships as he explored Asia.

The Russians faced large popular revolts from the Poles in 1830 (shown here) and 1863 and were unable to suppress Polish nationalism.

1830 and 1863, and the Russian state had to garrison Poland with thousands of troops to maintain control over the country. In Finland, attempts to impose Russian authority after 1890 met with a sustained campaign of civil disobedience from the Finns. The Caucasus continued to prove difficult for Russian officials to control.

Russia consistently took the view that its empire was a single state, to be governed by a consistent set of laws. The regime was very reluctant to recognize that its domains constituted colonies and that they should be treated differently to the Russian heartland of the state. The rise of nationalism during the 19th century did not leave Russia unscathed, and Ukrainians, Jews and the Baltic peoples all flexed their muscles. The Russian response was almost always to stamp out manifestations of national feeling. Russia's Jews suffered under severe restrictions on where they could live, access to education and the occupations that they could follow. When Ukrainian nationalist groups began to develop and assert a separate Ukrainian identity in the 1860s and 1870s, the Tsarist regime was quick to act. The Russian government prohibited the publication of anything in Ukrainian that was of a scholarly, religious or educational nature, effectively denying the existence of the Ukrainian language. In Poland, the Russians attempted to impose the use of the Russian language in schools, courts and local government. The Baltic provinces of the empire were also targeted for this policy of Russification: the university in Dorpat (present-day Tartu) was given a Russian name and teaching there had to take place in Russian. Land was offered to landless Orthodox peasants in the Baltic provinces to encourage conversions from Lutheranism and the quality of Orthodox schools was improved. The Russian regime recognized the importance of the Orthodox church in promoting imperial cohesion and gave the church special privileges, preventing other religions from opening new churches and establishing schools.

In little more than 150 years Russia was transformed from a regional northern European power to a mighty empire that bestrode Europe and Asia. Russian explorers, scientists and military men helped to build a state that exerted enormous influence and was able directly to confront Britain, the other great Asian imperial power. The Russian achievement in holding its vast and diverse empire

The Jewish population of the empire was largely confined to the Pale of Settlement, comprising parts of western Russia, Poland and Ukraine, although some (such as this family) lived in Central Asia. Quotas were imposed on Jewish access to education.

together was considerable, but the imperial state was based on the suppression of national and religious identities, as St Petersburg believed that the imposition of uniformity across the empire was the best way to cement its authority. It was a bold move to try to Russify this vast domain, especially since the state had only limited bureaucratic resources at its disposal. But Russia's ambition to become a global power drove its officials and soldiers to take extraordinary steps to impose Russian authority. St Petersburg found that it was not an easy task to restrain nationalist sentiment and activity: when revolution broke out in 1905, there were uprisings by national groups in the areas where Russification had been most intense. The regime was able to put down the revolts by using the most severe repression, despatching detachments of armed Cossacks to the Baltic provinces, one of the most rebellious regions. This gave only a short-term respite. When the Bolshevik regime came to power in 1917, most of the peoples that had been conquered by the Russians took advantage of the confusion to declare their independence.

This ethnographic map of Asiatic Russia was made by the great explorer Mikhail Veniukov and shows the variety of peoples that the empire incorporated.

OPPOSITE This pictorial map of Russia was produced for the 1896 All-Russia Exhibition of Industry and Art.

Chapter 5

Reform and Reaction, 1850–1900

In 1856, Russia lost the Crimean War. This catastrophe was to shape the remaining decades of Tsarism. In sharp contrast to the triumph over Napoleon, Russia was defeated on its own soil in the Crimea by British and French troops. Military disaster forced the Russian elite into a period of deep introspection as they sought to explain why their armies had been humbled. For more enlightened Russians, military defeat was the inevitable consequence of decades of refusal to reform, and it was Russian backwardness – its most obvious symbol being the continuing existence of serfdom – that had led the Romanov state to calamity. Tsar Nicholas I died in 1855 while the war was at its height, and his successor Alexander II (1855–81) recognized that change was essential if Russia was to regain its military status as a Great Power. Reform was not an easy option, however: military defeat had

OPPOSITE Issued in 1911 to commemorate the 50th anniversary of the emancipation of the serfs, the picture shows Alexander II surrounded by his grateful people.

A French cartoon of landowners gambling with bundles of serfs. Such lampooning of Russian serfdom increased the pressure for emancipation.

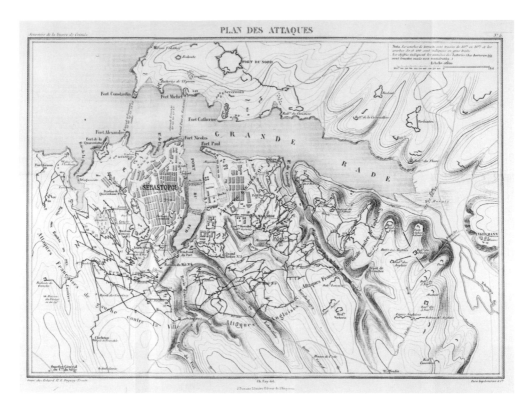

The siege of Sevastopol during the Crimean War had a disastrous outcome for the Russians. This map shows the battle lines: English in red, French in blue and the Russian defenders in green.

Sevastopol was devastated during the year-long siege: the fall of the city in September 1855 effectively ended the war.

emptied the Russian treasury and severe financial pressures gave the regime little room for manoeuvre. The most pressing issue facing Alexander II was serfdom. His advisers were almost unanimous that Russia's peasants had to be emancipated, but were they to be given land along with their freedom or simply transformed into landless agricultural workers? This exemplified the central dilemma faced by the Tsars: how far would reform undermine the social foundations of their regime? Although emancipating the peasants with land seriously weakened the power of the Russian nobility, Alexander II

It is better to abolish serfdom from above, rather than wait for the peasants to begin to abolish it from below. Tsar Alexander II, 1856[1]

decided that a landless peasantry posed such a serious potential for rebellion that the interests of the nobility could not prevail.

The 1861 emancipation of the serfs was the first of a series of reforms that, over the next decade, began to transform Russia into a modern state. Alexander II's Great Reforms included reform of the legal system, the introduction of jury trials for the first time, and proper payment for judges so that they did not need to take bribes. Education in both schools and universities was improved by establishing a more modern curriculum and relaxing some of the centralized controls that Nicholas I had put in place. Censorship of books and the press was eased a little. The system of conscription to the army underwent major reform, so that ordinary troops spent only six years in the regular army, instead of the effective service for life that had been the fate of serf-soldiers. And, for the first time, some Russians were given the opportunity to cast a vote to elect people who would govern them. Elected councils were established in most of rural European Russia and in the empire's largest towns and cities (albeit with a limited franchise that restricted the influence that the peasantry could exert and gave Russia's nobles disproportionately greater power). These councils – the *zemstvo* in the countryside, *dumas* in the cities – came to play a vital part in the provision of services such as health and education, levying their own taxation and bringing significant numbers of educated people to work in Russia's provinces.

Alexander II's reforms seemed to indicate that Russia was turning towards Europe and the Russian intelligentsia, emboldened

'Alexander II, Emperor and Autocrat of All the Russias' reads the inscription on this 1856 coronation medal.

Zemstvo

The *zemstvo* – the elected local councils established in 1864 across the Russian countryside – ran schools, provided hospitals, built roads and bridges and gave agricultural advice to peasant farmers. In Tolstoy's *Anna Karenina*, Vronsky declares that he will 'consider it an honour to be elected to the *zemstvo*. It is so I can make a return for the advantages I enjoy as a landowner',[2] but not all nobles shared this positive view. The Tauride provincial governor, A.G. Kaznacheev, attacked the *zemstvo* as 'created for the personal benefit of its members and not for the population of the district'.[3] The *zemstvo* employed substantial numbers of professional people: two thirds of Russia's agronomists worked for local councils and they ran 2,000 hospitals and more than 40,000 schools. During World War I the Union of *Zemstvo* and Union of Towns played a critical role in helping to supply Russia's army with equipment: the first Prime Minister of the 1917 Provisional Government was Georgii Lvov, who had chaired the *zemstvo* union.

The chart shows that by 1903, the zemstvo *contributed 22 per cent of national spending on primary education.*

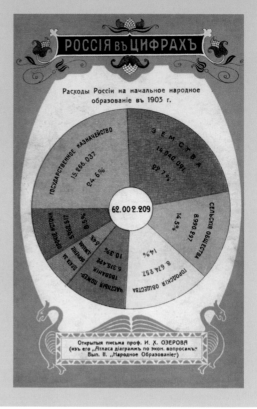

by the expansion of education and the greater opportunities for employment that Russia's new councils offered, believed that they could now press for even more wide-ranging changes. However, the Tsar himself quickly lost his enthusiasm for reform, a process that was accelerated by the growth in violent opposition to his regime. In 1866, Alexander II was deeply shocked when Dmitrii Karakozov attempted to assassinate him, and this proved to be only the start of persistent attempts to bring down the regime by terrorism. Revolutionaries all agreed that Russia's autocratic government was evil and oppressive; they argued that the failure of the Romanovs to provide any form of national representative government showed that the Tsars were determined to hang on to their power at all costs. The introduction of the *zemstvo* had given some hope that the principle of elected government had begun to take root in Russia, but the Tsars set their faces against anything that would reduce their own power. Deprived of any parliamentary forum for expressing ideas and debating issues, and living in a state where political parties were prohibited, Russians who wanted to bring about radical change had only one outlet: revolution. Russia's revolutionaries were, in the main, members of the empire's social elite. The expansion of university education in the 1860s helped to create an intelligentsia that was overwhelmingly unsympathetic to the Tsarist regime. Only a small minority of the intelligentsia espoused violent action to try to topple the Romanovs, but the intellectual climate of Russia in the late 19th century fostered antipathy to Tsarism. Russian Populists – *Narodniki* – wanted to bring about a revolution that would result in the overthrow of Tsarism and the development of a state and society based on the peasantry. The Populists wanted Russia to follow its own traditions, rather than industrializing along Western lines, but they faced great difficulties in persuading the peasantry to espouse their views.

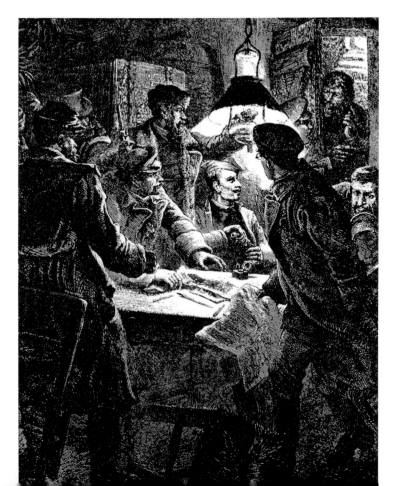

Russia's revolutionaries conspired to overthrow Tsarism from the 1870s onwards. This engraving of a group of Nihilists was published in *Harpers Weekly*.

Deprived of any means of mass communication with the over-whelmingly illiterate peasants, several hundred Populists attempted to 'Go to the People' in the early 1870s, heading off into the Russian countryside to spread the message of revolution. The campaign ended in utter failure. Some activists were handed over to the author-ities by the peasants and others found that their words simply fell on deaf ears.

From the 1870s, Russia was beset by violent attacks on members of the official elite. The governor of St Petersburg was shot and wounded in 1878, and – in a further challenge to the regime – a jury cleared the assailant of attempted murder. Vera Zasulich argued in her defence that her action was justified as she was attacking a tyran-nical regime; the jury's acceptance of her 'not guilty' plea infuriated the regime, while giving great encouragement to her comrades in the revolutionary movement. In April 1879 another attempt was made to assassinate the Tsar and this was followed, less than a year later, by a bombing in the Winter Palace itself, the very symbol of the Tsarist state and Alexander II's residence, which almost claimed his life. In March 1881, a terrorist cell finally succeeded in blowing Alexander II to pieces on the streets of his own capital city. The timing of the Tsar's murder was ironic: the turmoil of the late 1870s had persuaded

Tsar Alexander II was
assassinated by a terrorist
bomb when he stopped
his carriage to investigate
an earlier bombing.
He was taken to the
nearby Winter Palace,
where he died.

Alexander II to return to the reform agenda that had lain fallow for a decade. In early 1881 the Tsar had agreed to convene a national consultative assembly and he was preparing to sign this into law on the very day that he was assassinated.

The new Tsar, Alexander III, was deeply conservative by nature and this tendency was only reinforced by the violent death of his father. Any hopes that Russia's liberals entertained that the assassination might lead to further liberalization were dashed immediately. Alexander and his chief adviser, the reactionary and embittered Konstantin Pobedonostsev, imposed a state of emergency across much of European Russia, abandoned plans to introduce a consultative national assembly, and tried to reverse some of the reforms of the 1860s. It proved impossible to eradicate the spirit of the reforms from Russian society, however: the emancipation of the serfs had begun the process of inculcating a different view of humanity into the Russian people. Little by little, concepts of individual liberty and a taste for participation in the political process were taking hold. Attitudes changed only slowly, but ideas about legality and democracy

OPPOSITE Serov's 1900 portrait of Alexander III showed the Tsar's power and authority. Despite his deep conservatism, Alexander presided over an industrial boom and a Russian alliance with republican France.

Pobedonostsev

Konstantin Pobedonostsev (1827–1907) was one of the most influential Russian statesmen of the 19th century. Tutor to Alexander III and Nicholas II, he played a vital role in instilling conservative ideas into both men. Pobedonostsev came from an educated family and, while he had helped to draw up the legal reforms of the 1860s, he soon turned towards conservatism, believing that autocracy was the only way in which Russia could be ruled. Pobedonostsev's conservatism was arid and sterile: even his friends admitted that he had little constructive to offer. His *Reflections of a Russian Statesman* proceeded from the premise that humans were inherently sinful and must be constrained by a powerful state. He despised democracy as bogus and damaging, describing the concept of sovereignty of the people as 'the falsest of political principles'.[4] Ilya Repin's portrait of the dessicated Pobedonostsev encapsulated the intolerance and rigidity of the man, characteristics that helped increasingly to isolate Russia's conservatives from mainstream society.

Pobedonostsev, pictured by Repin at the centenary meeting of the Imperial State Council in 1902.

began to permeate Russian society during the later part of the 19th century. Alexander III tried to limit the powers of the elected local councils and to reduce the impact of the reformed judicial system by transferring controversial cases to military courts, but he could not silence calls for reform, calls that became ever more vociferous as the regime tried to restore its autocratic hold on Russia.

Nor could Alexander III eradicate revolutionary terrorism from Russia. Fearful for his own safety, he himself spent little time in his capital city, living instead in his well-protected country palace at Gatchina, 45 km (28 miles) south of St Petersburg. Even though the Russian state hunted down revolutionaries with great vigour and imposed severe punishments on those that were caught, revolution continued to attract adherents. In 1887 a plot to assassinate the Tsar was uncovered and its leaders were sentenced to death. One of the people executed was Alexander Ulianov, the older brother of the seventeen-year-old Vladimir who, during the 1890s, would become a committed Marxist and, taking the name Lenin, go on to bring the Bolsheviks to power in 1917.

Marxism gained influence in Russia at the end of the 19th century as industrialization took hold. Russia's defeat in the Crimean War exposed its economic weakness and the extent to which it had

Lenin sits in the centre of the League of Struggle for the Emancipation of the Working Class, just before his 1897 exile to Siberia.

fallen behind its Western European rivals. Industrial revolution had hardly taken hold in Russia and textiles remained the single largest industry. Supporters of Russian industrialization argued that military power depended on a powerful economy capable of sustaining a large army and equipping it with modern weaponry. The rapid technological advances of the 19th century strengthened this argument, as new types of artillery and rifles were produced. Yet it was not easy for Russia to industrialize. Russian agriculture did not produce large profits that could be invested in new industries, and there was no substantial and prosperous middle class with accumulated capital that could be tapped for investment. The Russian state's financial position was not strong enough for it to provide large-scale investment capital itself, so foreign investors were the only potential source of funding. Russia's unstable political situation made foreigners wary of pouring money into businesses there, and so industrial growth continued to be sluggish until the 1890s. In 1892, however, a new Minister of Finance took over: Sergei Witte had worked his way up through the railway industry and recognized the vital importance of transforming the Russian economy. He put in place a series of measures to enhance the appeal of Russia for foreign investors, taking Russia on to the gold standard in 1894 and raising customs duties so that it was advantageous to produce goods in Russia itself, rather than relying on imports. At the same time, he used the scarce financial resources of the Russian state to invest directly in railways, constructing more than 28,000 km (17,400 miles) of track between 1890 and 1905.

Witte's policies proved to be extremely successful: during the 1890s the Russian economy grew at an average of 8 per cent a year and foreign investment poured into Russia, especially from France and Germany. All the same, the development of Russian industry was not universally welcomed among the Russian governing elite. Industrialization brought with it urbanization, as millions of people poured into Russia's towns and cities to work in the burgeoning factories. By 1910 St Petersburg and Moscow were both among the ten largest cities in Europe, with populations of 2.1 million and 1.75 million respectively. The growth of a Russian working class posed a potential threat to the stability of the Tsarist regime: the Tsars had only to look at Western Europe to see how the advance of the

Sergei Witte (1849–1915) was one of Tsarist Russia's most influential statesmen. He directed economic policy during the 1890s and was instrumental in pushing through constitutional reform in 1905.

ABOVE A Bashkir switch operator poses by the Trans-Siberian railway, near the town of Ust' Katav in the Ural region of European Russia.

Russia's railways grew apace at the end of the 19th century, with more than 44,000 km (27,000 miles) of track in place by 1900.

Industrial Revolution unleashed widespread social and political unrest. Russia had escaped the Europe-wide revolutions of 1848, and for much of the Russian governing elite the chief priority was to maintain its unlimited authority. Social stability was the central concern for the Russian Ministry of Internal Affairs – responsible for the police – and it was deeply sceptical of the necessity for uncontrolled industrial growth. All the same, Witte's economic priorities prevailed: he insisted that Russia's imperial power depended on the growth of her industries. The Russian push to the Far East required the completion of the Trans-Siberian railway so that troops and supplies could be moved quickly to the Pacific coast. Witte argued that only rapid industrial growth could enable Russia to mount a proper challenge to threats to its eastern possessions.

Industrialization did help to promote social change in Russia. Migrants from the countryside came to work in Russia's cities, where living and working conditions were very poor. Long working hours, crowded housing and poor sanitation helped to provoke discontent and, in these circumstances, Marxism was able to gain adherents among the developing working class. While Populism had been based on Russia following its own historical traditions by developing a prosperous peasant-based economy and society, Marxism was unashamedly Western in its aims. Lenin's Russian Social Democratic party promoted proletarian revolution and its

Metal workshops were an essential part of Russian industrial growth, producing machinery for a wide variety of industries.

ideas proved to hold great appeal for the new Russian working class. Tsarist Russia found it difficult to cope with the challenges presented by defeat in war. Conservative structures were deeply ingrained in the fabric of state and society and reform had been delayed for too long. The most dramatic change after 1850 – the emancipation of the serfs – satisfied nobody: the nobility complained that they were being cast aside by the regime, while the peasantry resented having to make annual payments for the land that they had received. Russia's reformers wanted to go further and to move towards involving society in national government: in 1865 the Moscow assembly of the nobility urged Alexander II to meet with its representatives 'to deliberate on the general needs of the empire'.[5] The implication of their request was clear; they wanted to establish that they had a formal right to be consulted about the way in which Russia was to be governed. Alexander II's response to their request was robust. He wrote to them that: 'The right of initiative…belongs

'Land and liberty' is the best expression of the people's views on the ownership of land and the organization of society. Programme of Land and Liberty, 1878[6]

exclusively to me, and is indissolubly bound to the autocratic power entrusted to me by God'.[7]

Conservatives were frightened by the experience of reform during the 1860s and believed that Russia should remain true to its own traditions and reject the Western European model of political and economic reform. In the wake of Alexander II's assassination, the leading conservative statesman, Konstantin Pobedonostsev, argued that Russia 'was strong because it was an autocracy, because of the unlimited mutual trust and the close ties between the people and their Tsar'. He attacked the emancipation of the serfs, when 'the peasants had been given freedom, but without proper authority being established over them' and condemned the new elected councils as 'talking-shops, full of worthless, immoral men'.[8] Tensions inside Russian society grew sharper at the end of the 19th century as the regime entrenched itself, and opposition to the Tsarist state grew more strident. The industrial revolution promoted by Witte produced social and political consequences that were to be deeply unpalatable to the Romanov regime.

OPPOSITE Poverty was endemic in the cities of Imperial Russia. Unemployed men had to resort to soup kitchens such as this one on Vasilievskii Island in St Petersburg.

КНЯЗЬ ИГОРЬ

ОПЕРА
въ IV дѣйствіяхъ
съ прологомъ

слова и музыка
А. П. БОРОДИНА.

СЮЖЕТЪ
заимствованъ изъ

Слова
О полкѹ
ИГОРЕВѢ

Chapter 6

The Flowering of Russian Culture

Tsarist Russia was a cultural paradox. When the first empire-wide census was taken in 1897, only 21 per cent of the population were literate. In the countryside, many more men than women could read and write: even in the highly-industrialized Moscow province, more than half of men were literate, but only a quarter of women. Primary education never became universal or compulsory in Imperial Russia, and the best that most children could hope for was two years of rudimentary education. Yet at the same time, Russian culture attained exceptional creative heights and Russian writers, painters and composers produced a sustained outpouring of works that were quickly recognized as being of universal significance.

Russian school education was disorganized and uncoordinated until late in the 19th century. Peter the Great had wanted to expand education to guarantee Russia's national strength, but the new schools that opened in the first part of the 18th century took no

OPPOSITE Borodin's *Prince Igor* was first published in 1888. The stylized old Russian of its title page showed how the opera reached back into Russia's history.

More children – both boys and girls – were able to attend primary school after 1900, but access to secondary and higher education in Russia remained very limited.

pupils from the peasantry, instead concentrating on educating the sons of officials, soldiers and priests. Many different official bodies sponsored the establishment of schools: the Ministry of Education controlled some schools, but the Ministry of State Domains, the Ministry of Internal Affairs and the Mining Department also had their own schools. The Orthodox church was also an important provider of education but, despite this multiplicity of schools, the number of children who received education remained very small. Although the number of pupils increased from 62,000 in 1801 to 675,000 in 1869 and the number of schools grew tenfold during the same period, fewer than 5 per cent of Russian children received any education before the 1860s. Alexander II's Great Reforms provided a huge stimulus to education: the government itself invested more heavily in education, while the elected local councils – the *zemstvo* – took up the task of building schools with great enthusiasm. By 1911, more than 40 per cent of Russian school-age children were enrolled at school and in some provinces – notably Moscow – over 75 per cent of children received some education. Secondary and university education was much more limited in its availability. Only 70,000 Russians were enrolled in universities and higher education institutes in 1913, and more than 35 per cent of them were from the families of nobles, bureaucrats and military officers. The Tsarist educational system was making advances by the beginning of the 20th century, but was still far from providing the universal primary education that was becoming common in Western Europe.

The expansion of education and literacy was crucial in the development of Russian written culture. A Russian literary language hardly existed before 1700 and there was little hint, even in the 18th century, of the artistic riches that were to come over the following century. The foundations of Russian literary culture were laid by the poet Alexander Pushkin during the 1820s and 1830s. His poetry encompassed many different genres, ranging from intimate love poems to the great historical epic *The Bronze Horseman*, which took as its central motif the colossal equestrian statue of Peter the Great that stands in the centre of St Petersburg. Pushkin's genius extended far beyond his poetry: he also wrote prose and plays and he was responsible almost single-handedly for creating the Russian literary

OPPOSITE Watercolour portrait by Konstantin Somov of Alexander Pushkin at his desk.

LEFT Falconet's 1782 statue of Peter the Great – *The Bronze Horseman* – stands on Senate Square in St Petersburg, adjacent to the pre-revolutionary Senate and Holy Synod.

PETRO PRIMO
CATHARINA SECUNDA

Tolstoy

The greatest of Russia's novelists, Leo Tolstoy (1828–1910), was a member of the empire's social elite. Count Tolstoy owned a great estate at Yasnaya Polyana in the Tula countryside, south of Moscow, as well as a grand house in Moscow itself. He served as an army officer in the 1850s, fighting in the Crimean War, and this experience was reflected in his *Sebastopol Sketches*. Tolstoy wanted to show the reality of Russian life in his writing, and his two epic novels, *War and Peace* and *Anna Karenina*, each reflected some of the pressing social issues of the mid-19th century. Tolstoy idealized the Russian peasant, and his lyrical description of the harvest in *Anna Karenina* was intended to show the close bond that existed between Russians and their native land. For the last thirty years of his life Tolstoy focused on religious themes in his writings, embracing the concept of non-violence, and communities grew up that followed his teachings. In 1910 he abandoned his home and wealth, intending to live the simple life that he preached, but he quickly became ill and died at the country railway station of Astapovo.

Leo Tolstoy is portrayed barefoot and wearing peasant attire in Repin's 1901 portrait. Tolstoy's death in 1910 caused large popular demonstrations of sympathy in Russia.

language. He wrote in stylish and straightforward Russian, and the variety of types of work that he produced made his writings accessible to a wide audience. His verse novel, *Evgenii Onegin*, represented perhaps his greatest achievement, made even more popular by Tchaikovsky's opera.

While Pushkin's literary merit was exceptional, he also represented another vital tradition in Russian high culture through his sympathy with radical social and political ideas. Pushkin's connection with men who were involved in the Decembrist revolt made him a figure of deep suspicion to the authorities. He was exiled to his country estates in the 1820s and Nicholas I himself took an interest in the publication of Pushkin's works.

Pushkin was only the first of a remarkable procession of writers whose novels, plays and poetry brought Russian culture to the forefront of world literature. Over the next seventy years Leo Tolstoy and Fyodor Dostoyevsky wrote their great novels, Ivan Turgenev penned his stories and novels and Anton Chekhov's short stories and plays appeared in print. A host of other writers – Nikolai Gogol, Ivan Goncharov, Mikhail Lermontov, Fyodor Tiutchev and Afanasy Fet – also published works that were read widely and were of great significance.

Chekhov and Tolstoy in the Crimea in 1901. Chekhov's short stories and tersely-constructed plays contrasted with Tolstoy's more expansive writings.

Dostoyevsky's penetrating psychological portrait of Raskolnikov in *Crime and Punishment* and the challenging philosophical arguments of the Grand Inquisitor in *The Brothers Karamazov* contrast with the panoramic view of humanity that Tolstoy gives in both *War and Peace* and *Anna Karenina*.

Educated Russians read this great torrent of literature with huge enthusiasm, subscribing in large numbers to the so-called 'thick journals' such as *The Russian Messenger* in which novels often first appeared. Literature fulfilled a vital role in imperial Russia. Open political debate was largely impossible for Russians, political parties

All happy families are alike; each unhappy family is unhappy in its own way.

The opening line of Tolstoy's *Anna Karenina*[1]

were illegal before 1905 and discussion of anything that could be construed as an attack on the autocratic system was risky. Censorship of the press – even though it was relaxed a little in 1865 – remained a very powerful deterrent to the free expression of opinion. In such circumstances, literature came, in some ways, to provide a safe medium for debate about social and political issues that could not otherwise be aired openly. Fiction could offer reflections on the nature of political power – for example, Tolstoy's discussion of

Tolstoy's *War and Peace* was lauded in Tsarist Russia. This illustration for a 1932 Soviet edition showed how the book was celebrated even after the 1917 revolution.

Dostoyevsky's tortured and complex character emerges in this penetrating 1872 portrait by Vasilii Perov.

Napoleon in *War and Peace* – and of social issues such as serfdom. When Turgenev's *Notes of a Hunter* was published in 1852, it was judged by the authorities to be a direct assault on the morality of serfdom and the author was promptly exiled to his country estate.

Not all Russian writers were radicals, however. In the 1840s, the young Dostoyevsky became a member of the underground Petrashevsky circle, a small group of liberal intellectuals. The 1848 revolutions in Europe prompted Tsar Nicholas I to clamp down on any potential opposition and Dostoyevsky was arrested and sentenced to death. Saved from execution at the last moment, he was exiled to Siberia and spent four years there. Dostoyevsky's experiences prompted him to reconsider his liberal opinions and he turned towards Orthodox Christianity, rejecting revolution as a means of improving Russia's lot and instead promoting native Russian ideals. Speaking in 1880, Dostoyevsky stressed the uniqueness of the

Icons were almost the only form of painting in Russia from the conversion to Orthodox Christianity of Grand Prince Vladimir in 988 until the time of Peter the Great. Their style and function was very different from European art: they were intended to assist in worship and many icons became renowned for miracle-working and were carried into battle by campaigning armies. Icon painting followed rigid conventions, and icons depicted Biblical figures and scriptural scenes, with little originality in content or form. Many icons had richly decorated frames, adorned with precious metals and jewels, and they were used in Orthodox churches to cover the iconostasis, the screen that separated the body of the church from the sanctuary and altar. Few icon painters gained any individual fame: the best known artist was Andrei Rublev (*c.*1360–*c.*1429) whose *Trinity* was painted for the Trinity-Sergiev monastery at Zagorsk.

Andrei Rublev's Trinity, *regarded as one of the finest achievements of Russian painting.*

Russian soul, declaring that the 'destiny of a Russian is pan-European and universal'.[2] His semi-mystical view of Russia drew on the Slavophile tradition that suggested that Russia should follow its own path of historical development, rather than copying Western models. Dostoyevsky's later novels were heavily influenced by his religious beliefs and he attacked the nihilism of Russian revolutionaries.

Literature had an explicitly social purpose in Russian before 1900 and all serious writers, whatever their political views, understood that their task was not simply to provide entertainment. This view of the purpose of art extended beyond literature into the visual arts. Russian painting in the 18th and early 19th centuries was dominated by the 'Academy' style: formal art that drew on Western traditions and had few recognizably Russian elements. In the middle of the 19th century this was challenged by a new generation of painters who took their inspiration from explicitly national Russian themes and were intent on using their pictures to address social issues. Taking their name from the travelling exhibitions where they exhibited their works, the Itinerants produced pictures that reflected

OPPOSITE Miasoedov's *The Zemstvo is Dining* (1872) was an important piece in the realist tradition of Russian art. Its criticism of the *zemstvo* hit home hard.

Russian reality and, at the same time, challenged Russian society to confront some of its most difficult issues. Ivan Shishkin's forest scenes penetrated into the heart of the Russian psyche by portraying the archetypal Russian landscape, a wilderness that clearly demonstrated Russia's differences from its European neighbours and the prowess of the Russians who had tamed it.

Most of the Itinerants' works were far more hard-hitting, however, depicting the harshness of life for ordinary Russians in both town and country. Vladimir Makovsky's pictures of Moscow street-life showed the wretched poverty in which many Russians existed, while Grigory Miasoedov's *The Zemstvo is Dining* suggested that Russia's elected local councils placed scant importance on the interests of their constituents. These realist painters could also address explicitly political topics in their art: Isaac Levitan is best known for his almost dreamy landscape pictures of rural Russia, but among them is *The Vladimirka*, which shows an empty country road disappearing into the distance across a flat open plain. For Russians, however, this apparently innocuous piece of landscape painting was a picture of immense political significance. The *Vladimirka* – the

Shishkin's majestic forest paintings reminded Russians of their national identity. This one, titled simply *Forest*, was painted in 1892.

PREVOUS PAGES *The Vladimirka* – stretching forlornly away into the distance – was the road to Siberia for Russian political exiles. (Isaac Levitan, 1892)

The Volga Bargehaulers was one of the most startling pieces of art produced in Tsarist Russia. It showed the degradation of ordinary working men alongside Russia's iconic River Volga.

Vladimir road – was the route that political prisoners took on their way to exile in Siberia. Levitan's picture was a reminder of the brutal nature of the Tsarist regime under which all Russians lived.

The most significant Russian painter of the late 19th century was Ilya Repin. His work encompassed a very wide variety of subjects, ranging from his 1873 depiction of the *Volga Bargehaulers* to his 1886 picture of Tsar Alexander III meeting peasant village elders. Repin was not afraid to portray the harsh realities of Russian life in paintings such as *Religious Procession in Kursk Province*, which showed the devotion of the Russian people to the Orthodox faith, but also gave real insights into the nature of peasant society. Repin's work was highly valued by the Russian establishment and he was invited to paint the official picture marking the centenary of the State Council. His 1903 portrayal of the political elite of the Russian empire gathered at the council's centenary meeting, resplendent in their official uniforms, encapsulated Russian nationalist sentiment but, even here, Repin was able to give penetrating individual portrayals of the men who ruled the empire. His picture of *17 October 1905* also appealed to national

feeling, with its happy crowd demonstrating in support of the manifesto that established the Duma, but the red banners that were being carried by the marchers showed that the political tide was turning.

Russia was also one of the great centres of classical music during the 19th century, and its composers worked in a distinctive Russian style. Mikhail Glinka began the process with his 1836 opera *A Life for the Tsar*, its title suggesting the patriotic themes that permeated the work. Glinka's nationally-oriented music helped to give birth to a broad tradition of Russian classical music that drew heavily on folk song and on eastern elements. Vladimir Stasov, the most influential Russian critic during the late 19th century, wrote that folk song was a vital part of Russian identity:

> Every peasant, every carpenter, every mason, every yardman, every coachman, every old woman, every laundress and cook, every nanny and wet-nurse brings folk songs with them from their own region to Petersburg and Moscow…Every working man and woman in Russia gets on with his work singing folk songs. The Russian soldier goes into battle with them on his lips.[3]

Engraving of 1845 showing Mikhail Glinka (1804–57) at the piano. His operas and orchestral pieces became the mainstay of the Russian musical repertoire.

As Stasov recognized, most Russian composers were brought up in the provinces and had close contact with the folk melodies of ordinary Russian people. The work of Modest Mussorgsky, Alexander Borodin and Nikolai Rimsky-Korsakov reflected the rhythms and cadences of Russia's traditional music, reminding Russians of the roots of their national identity. At the same time, Russian composers worked eastern themes into their music. Glinka and Mily Balakirev both visited the Caucasus, but the acquisition of Russia's Asian empire during the 19th century and the wide attention paid to the culture of the new domains brought eastern timbres into the mainstream of Russian music. Glinka wrote that 'our Russian song is the child of the north but has been passed on by the inhabitants of the east'[4] and his own compositions showed the influence of Russia's Asian cultures.

During the late 1850s and 1860s, a group of five composers formed an informal group that became known as 'The Mighty Handful'. Balakirev, Borodin, Mussorgsky, Rimsky-Korsakov and Cesar Cui aimed to produce a national Russian music, far removed

Theatres in Tsarist Russia began as the preserve of the imperial court. In 1756 the Alexandrinksii theatre in St Petersburg was established and its stage witnessed the first performances of many of Russia's greatest plays: Chekhov's *Seagull*, Gogol's *Inspector-General* and Alexander Griboedov's *Woe from Wit* all had their premieres there. The Marinskii theatre was founded in 1783, and new Russian operas were regularly performed on its vast stage. Mussorgsky's *Boris Godunov*, Borodin's *Prince Igor* and Tchaikovsky's *Queen of Spades* were each first presented to the St Petersburg public. In Moscow, the Bolshoi and the Maly theatres were both under the control of the imperial court. The imperial theatres were subsidized by the government and were expected to stage productions using the best of Russia's actors. In the 1880s the imperial theatre's monopoly on the performance of plays, opera and ballet in St Petersburg was lifted, allowing the opening of a whole series of new theatres in the two capitals.

Fedor Chaliapin (1873–1938) was one of Russia's greatest opera singers (bass). This painting by Alexander Golovin (1912) shows him in the role of Boris Godunov.

from the classical traditions that were the mainstay of the St Petersburg Conservatoire. The music of 'The mighty handful' paralleled the paintings of the Itinerants in its focus on the Russian people and emphasis on the significance of Russia's heritage in its national identity. St Petersburg was a magnet for European musicians: the St Petersburg Philharmonia was founded in 1802 and the great figures of European music performed in its concert hall. Liszt, Berlioz, Wagner, Mahler and Schumann all conducted there, but at the begin-

There is a sort of fundamental good humour in the Imperial theatres, an unaffected pleasure in the theatre as it is with the conventional applause, bows, bouquets, suppers, newspaper criticism and all the rest. H.W. Williams, British observer of Russia, 1914[5]

ning of the 20th century the Russian capital became the focus for radical changes in artistic culture.

Russian writers, artists and musicians began to move away from the fiercely national themes that had dominated Russian culture since the 1850s and a much more heterogeneous artistic culture developed. Artists rebelled against the idea that art had to convey a social message, believing instead that art was valuable for its own sake. The World of Art movement acted as the stimulus for new departures in all forms of artistic endeavour. Poetry was a vital part of

Anton Chekhov (1860–1904) reading his play *The Seagull* to the Moscow Art Theatre company. The first performance of the play was greeted with loud booing.

The *World of Art* movement was a radical departure in the Russian artistic world, providing a focus for symbolist and aesthetic tendencies in what became known as Russia's Silver Age.

OPPOSITE Léon Bakst (1866–1924) was a prominent member of *World of Art* and designed costumes for Stravinsky's *Firebird*.

this movement. Anna Akhmatova, Alexander Blok and Nikolai Gumilev wrote poems that reflected the atmosphere of greater freedom engendered by the tumult of 1905. The greatest impact of the artistic revolution came on the stage, with the 1909 establishment of the Ballets Russes. The first performance of Igor Stravinsky's *Firebird* in 1910 marked a new era in European music and dance, while Russian painters were also instrumental in the creation of the abstract art that dominated 20th-century visual culture. The work of Natalia Goncharova played a vital role in the development of Futurism, as Russia's artists involved themselves in the Europe-wide debates about the fate of the old regime, their revolutionary abstract works paralleling the political revolution that was fomenting in Russian society. The publication in 1913 of the Russian Futurist manifesto *A Slap in the Face of Public Taste* showed how far the artistic revolution had gone: its authors declared that 'The Academy and Pushkin are less intelligible than hieroglyphics. Throw Pushkin, Dostoevsky, Tolstoy, etc., etc. overboard from the Ship of Modernity.'[6] Vladimir Mayakovsky, one of the signatories of the manifesto, became a stalwart supporter of the Bolsheviks after the 1917 October revolution.

BAKST
1910

oiseau de feu

Chapter 7

The End of Tsarism

In 1894, Alexander III died unexpectedly from kidney disease at the age of forty-nine. His son, the new Tsar Nicholas II, told Grand Duke Alexander Mikhailovich that:

> I am not prepared to be a Tsar. I never wanted to become one. I know nothing of the business of ruling. I even have no idea how to talk to the ministers.[1]

Contemporaries noted that he appeared almost lost in the hubbub that accompanied his father's funeral obsequies and his own accession. Count Lambsdorff, later to become Foreign Minister, commented that: 'His Majesty still lacks the external appearance and manner of an emperor'.[2] But the new Tsar did feel sure of his own mission. Nicholas promised to follow the path his father had laid out: this was not just empty rhetoric, but stemmed from Nicholas's deep respect and admiration for Alexander III, both as a father and as Tsar. In political terms, he wanted to continue the policies that his father had pursued and which, in Nicholas's view, had brought stability to the empire. Indeed, Nicholas knew no other way of ruling.

The new Tsar continued to oppose reform, brushing aside calls for change as 'senseless dreams'.[3] In 1905, however, the Romanovs were faced with a severe threat to their authority. Convinced of the strength of their armed forces, the Russians declared war on Japan in 1904, sure that they would win a quick and easy victory. They were wrong: the Japanese proved to be formidable opponents and Russia

Painted the year after his accession to the throne, this portrait of Nicholas II by Ilya Repin conveys the new Tsar's youth and inexperience.

OPPOSITE Parts of the Winter Palace were converted into a hospital during World War I.

This Russian cartoon of the 1904–05 Russo-Japanese War shows Russian troops triumphing, but the reality was very different. Japan inflicted a comprehensive defeat on Russia.

suffered humiliating reverses both on land and at sea. The main Russian land base at Port Arthur was captured in January 1905, while at sea the Russian Baltic fleet sailed halfway round the world, only to be sunk by the Japanese at Tsushima in May 1905. Russia erupted in revolution while the war was in progress: in January 1905 a peaceful march in St Petersburg by working people was dispersed by troops opening fire on the demonstrators. Hundreds were killed, and 'Bloody Sunday' sparked off a great wave of strikes and demonstrations as Russian workers took to the streets to show their anger with

A Tsar that is meek and humble...will see his realm impoverished and his glory diminished. A Tsar that is feared and wise will see his realm enlarged...A realm without dread is like a horse... without a bridle. Ivan Peresvetov, Lithuainian nobleman, 1549[4]

the Tsarist regime. More than 400,000 people struck in January and February, prompting the government to send mounted Cossacks into Russia's cities to put down the rebellions. The crisis facing the Russian state intensified as the countryside too broke out in open revolt. Russia's peasants took advantage of the weakness of the regime to seize land and burn manor houses, and the government had to despatch troops on more than 3,000 separate occasions to put down rural revolts. As the threat to the regime grew more severe,

ABOVE 'Bloody Sunday' –
9 January 1905 – marked
the beginning of a year
of unrest, with strikes
and demonstrations
against Tsarism.

Hundreds of thousands
of workers came out on
strike during 1905,
demanding better working
conditions and, increasingly,
wider reforms.

The 1905 mutiny on the battleship *Prince Potemkin*. In 1925, Eisenstein's dramatic film would portray the mutineers as heroic figures fighting against Tsarist oppression.

Russia's liberal intelligentsia grew very vocal in its demands for reform, seizing the opportunity to call for limitations on the power of the Tsar and the introduction of a parliamentary system. The pressure on Nicholas II and his ministers was heightened by rebellions among many of the empire's national minorities: Finns, Poles, Ukrainians and the Baltic peoples all rose up against their Russian masters. Worse still, and deeply dangerous to the Tsarist regime, elements of the armed forces mutinied. In June 1905 the crew of *Prince Potemkin*, a battleship stationed in the Black Sea, overthrew their officers and sailed the vessel to a Romanian port.

Under attack from all sides, the Tsarist regime was profoundly divided about how to respond to the developing revolution. Nicholas II and his closest advisers stood firmly against making any concessions to the rebels, believing that, as successive Tsars had done in the past, they could use force to assert their authority. But now there were powerful forces inside the Russian establishment opposing the Tsar's position. Sergei Witte led the demands for change, using his position as the successful negotiator of the peace treaty with Japan in August 1905 to press home the case for fundamental reform. By October of the same year, with strikes and rural unrest again threatening the survival of the regime, Nicholas II was persuaded to agree to reform. The October Manifesto promised an elected parliament – the Duma – and extended civil liberties, giving Russians freedom of speech and the right to hold meetings and to form associations and political parties. This was a remarkable volte-face for the Romanov regime, but Nicholas II never reconciled himself to the concessions that he had made, continuing to cling on to the belief that he remained an autocrat, able to govern as he wished.

The first elections to the new parliament took place early in 1906 and the Duma assembled in St Petersburg in April. It proved to be a radical and fractious body, demanding the compulsory seizure of noble-owned land and its redistribution to the peasantry, as well as calling for an amnesty for political prisoners. After six weeks, the government dissolved the Duma, but the Second Duma proved to be of much the same political complexion. The revolts that had dominated 1905 had been put down with great brutality by Tsarist troops and, emboldened by its success in restoring order to the Russian empire, the regime clawed back some of the political concessions it

The satirical magazine *Pulemet* ('Machine gun') showed Nicholas II's October Manifesto stained with blood.

Reaction to the October Manifesto among Russia's middle classes was enthusiastic, as Repin depicted in his painting *17 October 1905*.

The ceremonial opening of the First Duma in April 1906 showed the gulf between the wealth of Russia's elite and the humdrum existence of the peasant deputies.

had made. The Duma was counterbalanced in the legislative system by a reformed State Council, with half its members appointed directly by the Tsar (thus guaranteeing a conservative majority) and the Tsar himself also had to approve every piece of legislation. Radical reform could therefore be blocked. In June 1907, the government dissolved the Second Duma and, at the same time – and entirely unconstitutionally – changed the electoral system to reduce radical representation in the Duma.

Peter Stolypin had become Prime Minister in 1906, wanting both to pacify Russia and to make further social and economic reforms. His land reform allowed peasants to set up their own independent farms, separate from the village commune, but the outbreak of World War I brought the process to a halt. Stolypin also tried to introduce a set of reforms in other areas of Russian life: local government, education, the legal system and civil rights were all to be reformed, but opposition from the Right to his plans ensured that they failed. In 1911, Stolypin was assassinated in dubious circumstances, leaving a strong suspicion that his conservative opponents may have had a hand in his murder. Although social unrest continued after 1905, the Tsarist regime was able to maintain order, sometimes by force, as when workers at the Lena goldfields rebelled in 1912 and troops fired into the crowd, killing more than 100 men. The Duma had been emasculated by the changes to the franchise in 1907, and the centrist majority of the Third Duma caused few problems for the government. However, there were premonitions of disaster. Alexander Guchkov, leader of the centrist Octobrist party, warned in 1913 that the 'encroachment of reaction'[5] could lead to a protracted period of chronic anarchy, while Peter Durnovo, one of the most conservative members of the Russian political elite, predicted that a war with Germany would bring about a revolution that would sweep away the old order. These views went unheeded by the Tsar and his entourage. The Romanovs celebrated the centenary of Borodino in 1912 and the tercentenary of the dynasty in the following year, believing that they had reforged the link between sovereign and people that would keep them in power.

In summer 1914, Russia's international entanglements drew it into World War I. Allied to France since 1894, the Russians wanted to

The tercentenary of the Romanov dynasty in 1913 was marked by officially-sponsored celebrations that stressed the place of the monarchy in Russian national life.

This Romanov tercentenary Fabergé egg was given by Nicholas II to his wife as an Easter present in 1913. The egg is decorated with portraits of the Romanov rulers.

protect their Serbian brothers against the Austrians after the assassination of Archduke Franz Ferdinand. The complex balance of alliances drew Germany onto the Austrian side, facing Russia, France and Great Britain. Nicholas II was encouraged to go to war by his generals, who assured him that the vast Russian army would easily vanquish Germany and Austria. In fact, Russia's military performance proved to be dismal. In summer 1914, the Germans inflicted heavy defeats on Russia at the battles of Tannenberg and the Masurian Lakes and, while the Russians were able to make some headway against Austria-Hungary, in 1915 the Germans swept eastwards, occupying substantial areas of western Russia. The war had a dramatic impact on Russia's economy. The closure of Russian land frontiers with Germany and Austria-Hungary in 1914 deprived Russia of its largest trading partners, and foreign investment in Russian industry came to an abrupt halt. Russia's railway network was placed under huge stress, as it tried to transport millions of men

ABOVE AND LEFT Trench warfare was a feature of fighting on the Eastern Front during World War I. Conditions were miserable for Russian troops and the Bolsheviks were able to disseminate propaganda widely across the army.

to the front, along with food and equipment. As the war went on, the weather did not help. Tsar Nicholas II warned in February 1917:

> The snowstorms have put our armies in a critical position...if the movement of trains is not restored at once, real famine will break out among the troops in 3–4 days.[6]

(When rebellion broke out in Petrograd a few days later, demonstrators were urged to arm themselves with pieces of ice to use against Tsarist troops.) The process of transition to a war economy was slow and difficult, and Russian armaments production only began to reach the required levels late in 1915. The conscription of millions of men to fight in the armed forces deprived the countryside of young peasant farmers, meaning that women and the elderly had to work in the fields. The army also requisitioned horses from farmers, making agricultural work even more difficult. The system of

The army is disintegrating both morally and numerically...there is growing confusion at Headquarters. Retreat, retreat and retreat – that is all we hear from HQ.

A.A. Polivanov, Minister of War, July 1915[7]

exemption from conscription was not always effective, and Russia's factories also found that their labour force was depleted by the needs of the army.

Russian society was profoundly affected by the war: 700,000 men died on the battlefield between 1914 and 1917, more than 2.6 million Russian soldiers were wounded in combat and a further 2.5 million contracted disease during military service. During 1914 and 1915, as the Germans advanced, more than 6 million refugees flooded eastwards. The experience of the front was quickly transmitted to Russian civilians and the feeble performance of the Russian army helped to engender growing discontent with the Tsarist regime.

Russia's parliamentary politicians were excluded from the conduct of the war: the Duma met only infrequently and the government attempted to restrict its debates. In 1915, the majority of the Duma deputies established the Progressive Bloc and called for a 'responsible ministry',[8] a government that enjoyed the trust of the Duma. Still Nicholas II rejected all attempts by Russian society to

OPPOSITE 'Tsar, church and the rich on the shoulders of working people': Apsit's wartime drawing encapsulated the popular mood.

The Russian army suffered huge losses during World War I, and the way in which the regime dealt with the millions of wounded soldiers encapsulated some of the tensions in Russian society. The imperial family was quick to seize the opportunity to show itself as united with the Russian people: Empress Alexandra and her two eldest daughters, Olga and Tatiana, enrolled as nurses and were frequently photographed in nursing uniform alongside the wounded. Buildings at Tsarskoe Selo were converted into a hospital for the wounded and Grand Duchess Mariia Pavlovna, the Tsar's great-aunt, established her own organization to assist injured soldiers. It was important for the Romanovs to show that they were the protectors of the nation, and Mariia Pavlovna's relief committee set up workshops employing wounded soldiers to make clothing and footwear for the army.

Empress Alexandra in a nurse's uniform, photographed with her son Aleksei.

engage in the work of wartime government and, indeed, exacerbated the situation by himself taking on the job of Commander-in-Chief in August 1915, thus ensuring that Russia's weak military performance could be laid directly at his door. By the end of 1916, trust had completely broken down between the Tsarist regime and almost the entire political class. Furious at the behaviour of the government, Paul Miliukov, one of the leaders of the liberal Kadet party, spoke in the Duma in November 1916, cataloguing the failures of Tsarism in its prosecution of the war and asking 'Is this stupidity or treason?'[9]

Popular sentiment was inflamed by the scandals associated with Rasputin, a disreputable religious mystic who had wormed his way into the confidence of the imperial family. The Russian press ridiculed the Romanovs, portraying the German-born Empress Alexandra as plotting to defeat Russia, and making scurrilous insinuations about her relationship with Rasputin. The high hopes that the Tsar and his ministers had held in 1914 for a war that would unite Russia's people proved to be utterly false: by the end of 1916 Russian society was splintered and the regime was entirely isolated from the Russian people. At the end of February 1917, workers took to the streets of Petrograd – the capital's name had been changed in 1914 from the German-sounding St Petersburg – protesting at a shortage of bread. Russia's creaking railway system had proved unable to deliver grain supplies to the cities, while rapid inflation made the peasantry reluctant to grow grain for the open market. The demonstrations in Petrograd spread quickly, bringing out great crowds in open rebellion against the government. The regime ordered its troops to put down the revolt by force but, in contrast to 1905, it was clear that the Petrograd garrison would not open fire on the demonstrators. Events moved very quickly: Russia's Duma politicians and senior generals were in agreement that the only way to deal with the popular discontent was for the Tsar to abdicate. Nicholas II, isolated from Petrograd at army headquarters in Mogilev, 600 km (373 miles) from the capital, was cut off from most of his advisers and, very significantly, from his strong-willed wife. He accepted the advice to abdicate and gave up the throne less then ten days after the start of the rebellion in Petrograd. Three hundred years of Romanov rule ended with little more than a whimper.

Grigory Rasputin wielded considerable influence over the Empress. He was killed by a group of Russian aristocrats in December 1916 and his body flung into the freezing River Neva.

The Tsarist regime was replaced by a Provisional Government, initially dominated by liberal Duma politicians. The new government faced three central problems: Russia's continued involvement in World War I, food shortages and peasant demands for land reform. It failed to deal adequately with any of these pressing issues. Under strong pressure from its British and French allies, Russia continued to fight in the war, but this antagonized large sections of the Russian population who believed that Russia should pull its troops out. Continued rapid inflation meant that the peasantry could not be persuaded to increase grain production and food supply continued

We have deemed it Our duty to assist Our people to draw closer together and to unite all Our forces for the rapid achievement of victory. We have recognized the benefit of abdicating from the throne. Nicholas II, 2 March 1917[10]

to be unreliable. Last, the Provisional Government regarded itself as being merely a stop-gap until a Constituent Assembly was elected to determine Russia's permanent form of government and it was, therefore, unwilling to take major decisions on the land question. The Provisional Government was also confronted by Soviets of workers and soldiers: these bodies had emerged during the tumult of 1905 and they quickly reformed after the February revolution that had ejected Nicholas II from power. The Petrograd Soviet emerged as a serious rival to the Provisional Government and this 'dual power' constrained the actions of the government. The Soviet had particular influence among the army and its Order No. 1, issued immediately

The 1917 May Day demonstration in Petrograd took place in an atmosphere of euphoria, less than two months after the abdication of the Tsar. But the Bolsheviks were already planning to seize power.

The Fate of the Romanovs

After Nicholas II's abdication, he returned to the Alexander Palace at Tsarskoe Selo where he and his family had lived since 1895. But he was now under arrest and the family was confined to the palace and its park. The Provisional Government decided to move the Romanov family to Tobolsk in western Siberia in July 1917, far from the tumult of Petrograd. After the Bolshevik revolution, the position of the Romanovs became precarious and arguments developed among the Bolsheviks about the family's fate, with some advocating a full public trial for Nicholas. Events soon overtook the discussions. Civil war burst into life in early 1918, and in the confusion that ensued, the Romanovs were moved to Ekaterinburg in April. Worried that anti-Bolshevik forces might capture the family, Moscow ordered their execution. During the night of 16 July, the family was ordered into the basement of the building in which they were living and were shot and bayoneted to death. Their bodies were dumped down a mine-shaft and only identified in the 1990s.

Nicholas II under house arrest. The Romanovs hoped that they would find asylum in Britain, but the British government vetoed the plan, fearful of the possible domestic reaction.

The Bolsheviks formed their own military detachments in autumn 1917 and these troops seized power in Petrograd during the night of 25 October.

after the Tsar's abdication, instructed soldiers to obey their officers' orders only if the Soviet endorsed them.

During the spring and summer of 1917, Russia slipped towards anarchy. The Petrograd government's authority was weak and it proved unable to unite Russian society. The Provisional Government itself was unstable, with frequent changes of ministers, and it faced threats from both left and right. At the beginning of July, Lenin's Bolshevik party staged a half-hearted attempt to bring down the government, but they had insufficient support and the revolt petered out. In the following month General Kornilov began to march his troops towards Petrograd, determined to replace the Provisional Government with a military dictatorship. His soldiers were unwilling to support him and his rebellion too came to naught.

Lenin had returned to Russia from exile in Switzerland in April 1917 and the Bolshevik party stood alone in its opposition to the Provisional Government, a stance that bore fruit as the government's popularity shrank. By the autumn, Lenin and his lieutenants calculated that the Bolsheviks had sufficient support to try to seize power from the disunited and shambolic government. During the night of 25 October, armed Bolshevik detachments took control of key buildings in Petrograd, arresting most of the members of the Provisional Government in the Malachite Chamber of the Winter Palace. Tsarist Russia had been destroyed once and for all.

Resources

Chronology

1613 Election of Michael Romanov as first Romanov Tsar

1645 Death of Michael Romanov

1645–76 Reign of Tsar Aleksei

1676–82 Reign of Tsar Fyodor

1682–1725 Reign of Peter I the Great

1697–98 Peter's visit to the West

1700–21 Great Northern War with Sweden

1703 Peter the Great founds St Petersburg

1709 Russian victory over Charles XII of Sweden at Poltava

1721 Russia signs Treaty of Nystad with Sweden

1725–27 Reign of Catherine I

1727–30 Reign of Peter II

1730–40 Reign of Anna

1740–41 Reign of Ivan VI

1741–62 Reign of Elizabeth

1754–62 Bartolomeo Rastrelli builds the Winter Palace

1761–62 Reign of Peter III

1762–96 Reign of Catherine II the Great

1772 First partition of Poland

1773–75 Pugachev revolt

1793 Second partition of Poland

1795 Third partition of Poland

1796–1801 Reign of Paul I

1801–25 Reign of Alexander I

1809 Annexation of Finland

1812 Napoleon's invasion of Russia

1825–55 Reign of Nicholas I

1825 Decembrist revolt

1830–31 Polish rebellion

1837 Pushkin is shot in a duel and dies

1838 First Russian railway – St Petersburg to Tsarskoe Selo

1851 St Petersburg to Moscow railway opens

1853–56 Crimean War

1855–81 Reign of Alexander II

1861 Emancipation of the serfs

1863 Polish rebellion

1864–85 Conquest of Central Asia

1869 Tolstoy's *War and Peace*

1877 Tchaikovsky's *Swan Lake*

1877–78 War with Turkey

1880 Dostoevsky's *Brothers Karamazov*

1881–94 Reign of Alexander III

1891 Construction of the Trans-Siberian railway begins

1894–1917 Reign of Nicholas II

1897 First all-Russian census

1904–5 Russo-Japanese War

1905 1905 revolution

1906 First Duma

1907 Second Duma

Third Duma

1910 Death of Leo Tolstoy

1912 Fourth Duma

1914 Outbreak of World War I

St Petersburg is renamed Petrograd

1917 Abdication of Nicholas II

Formation of Provisional Government

October revolution

Notes

Introduction: The Russian Lands

1 Ivan Aksakov, *Pis'ma k rodnym 1844–1849 [Letters to my Relations, 1844–1849]*, Moscow 1988, p. 373.
2 Mikhail Bulgakov, *A Country Doctor's Notebook*, trans. Michael Glenny, London 1975, pp. 90–91.

Chapter 1 Peter the Great and the Westernization of Russia

1 Johann Vockerodt, *Rossiia pri Petre Velikom po rukopisnomu izvestiiu Ionna Gottgil'fa Fokkerodta [Russia under Peter the Great in the Manuscripts of Johann Gotthilf Vockerodt]*, St Petersburg 1874, p. 105.
2 Georg Grund, *Doklad o Rossii v 1705–1710 [Report on Russia 1705–1710]*, ed. Iu.N. Bespiatykh, St Petersburg 1992, p. 126.
3 J. Fennell (ed.), *Pushkin*, Harmondsworth 1964, p. 235.

Chapter 2 Russia's Rural World

1 Mikhail Bulgakov, *A Country Doctor's Notebook*, trans. Michael Glenny, London 1975, p. 41.
2 Olga Semyonova Tian-Shanskia, *Village Life in Late Tsarist Russia*, ed. David Ransel, Bloomington 1993, p. 119.
3 *Materialy dlia geografii i statistiki Rossii, Riazanskaia guberniia, [Materials on the Geography and Statistics of Russia, Riazan Province]*, St Petersburg 1860, p. 397.
4 B.N. Chicherin, *Vospominaniia. Zemstvo i Moskovskaia Duma [Memoirs. The Zemstvo and the Moscow City Council]*, Moscow 1934, p. 60.
5 A.N. Engel'gardt, *Iz derevni. 12 pisem, 1872–1887 [From the Country. 12 Letters 1872–1887]*, Moscow 1960, p. 124.

Chapter 3 The Tsars Triumphant, 1750–1850

1 W. Bruce Lincoln, *Nicholas I. Emperor and Autocrat of All the*

Russias, London 1978, p. 198.

2 A. de Custine, *La Russie en 1839*, vol. 2, Brussels 1843, p. 215.

3 Simon Dixon, *Catherine the Great*, London 2009, p. 304.

4 G. Vernadsky, *A Source Book for Russian History from Early Times to 1917*, vol. 2, New Haven 1972, p. 453.

5 L. Zakharova, 'Autocracy and the reforms of 1861–1874 in Russia. Choosing paths of development', in B. Eklof et al (eds), *Russia's Great Reforms, 1855–1881*, Bloomington 1994, p. 26.

Chapter 4 Building an Empire

1 A.I. Herzen, 'Eshche variatsiia na staruiu temu' [More variations on an old theme], *Sobrannie sochineniia, [Collected Works]* vol. 12, Moscow 1957, p. 426.

2 *Tobol'skii sever glazami politicheskikh ssyl'nykh XIX-nachalo XX veka [The Tobolsk North through the Eyes of Political Exiles in the 19th and Early 20th Centuries]*, Ekaterinburg 1998, p. 36.

3 Nikolai Przheval'skii, *Ot Kiakhty na istoki Zheltoi reki: issledovanie severnoi okrainy Tibeta i put' cherez Lob-nor po basseinu Tarima [From Kiakhta to the Source of the Yellow River: The Exploration of the Northern Boundary of Tibet and the Way across Lob-Nor along the Banks of the Tarim]*, St Petersburg 1888, p. 508.

4 N.F. Dubrovin, *Nikolai Mikhailovich Przheval'skii. Biograficheskii ocherk [N.M. Przheval'skii. Biographical Essay]*, St Petersburg 1890, p. 572.

Chapter 5 Reform and Reaction, 1805–1900

1 'Zapiska Senatora Ia.A. Solove'eva o krestiianskom dele' [Senator Ia.A. Solovev's note on the peasant question], *Russkaia starina [Russian Antiquity]*, vol. 30 (1881), p. 229.

2 Leo Tolstoy, *Anna Karenina*, trans. R. Peaver and L. Volokhonsky, London 2000, p. 633.

3 A.G. Kaznacheev, 'Mezhdu strokami odnogo formuliarnogo spiska', [Between the lines of one service record] *Russkaia starina [Russian Antiquity]*, vol. 32 (1881), p. 859.

4 K.P. Pobedonostsev, *Reflections of a Russian Statesman*, London 1898, p. 32.

5 A.A. Kornilov, *Obshchestvennoe dvizhenie pri Aleksandre II. (1855–1881). Istoricheskie ocherki [The Social Movement in the Reign of Alexander II. (1855–1881). Historical Essays]*, Moscow 1909, p. 172.
6 *Revoliutsionnoe narodnichestvo 70-kh godov XIX veka [Revolutionary Populism of the 1870s]*, vol. 2, Moscow-Leningrad 1965, p. 31.
7 T. Emmons, *The Russian Landed Gentry and the Peasant Emancipation of 1861*, Cambridge 1968, pp 410–11.
8 B.S. Itenberg and V.A. Tvardovskaia (eds), *Graf M. T Loris-Melikov i ego sovremenniki [Count M. T. Loris-Melikov and his Contemporaries]*, Moscow 2004, p. 574.

Chapter 6 The Flowering of Russian Culture

1 Leo Tolstoy, *Anna Karenina*, trans. R. Peaver and L. Volokhonsky, London 2000, p. 3.
2 F.M. Dostoyevsky, *Polnoe sobranie sochinenii v tridtsati tomakh [Complete Works in Thirty Volumes]*, vol. 26, Moscow 1984, p. 147.
3 V.V. Stasov, 'Nasha muzyka za poslednie 25 let russkogo isskustva' [Our music over the last 25 years of Russian art], *Vestnik Evropy [Herald of Europe]*, vol. 103 (1883), p. 566.
4 M.I. Glinka, *Zapiski [Notes]*, Leningrad 1953, p. 108.
5 H.W. Williams, *Russia of the Russians*, London 1914, p. 270.
6 V. Markov (ed.), *Manifesty i programmy futuristov [Futurist Manifestos and Programmes]*, Munich 1967, p. 50.

Chapter 7 The End of Tsarism

1 Alexander Mikhailovich, *Once a Grand Duke*, New York 1932, p. 169.
2 V.N. Lamzdorf, *Dnevnik 1894–1896 [Diary 1894–1896]*, Moscow 1991, p. 89.
3 D. Lieven, *Nicholas II. Emperor of all the Russias*, London 1993, p. 71.
4 *Chteniia obshchestva istorii i drevnosti Moskovskogo universiteta [Readings of the Moscow University Society of History and Antiquities]*, vol. 2, pt. 1, Moscow 1908, p. 70.
5 A.I. Guchkov, 'The general political situation and the Octobrist

party', *Russian Review*, vol. III (1914), no. 1, p. 151.

6 C.E. Vulliamy, *The Letters of the Tsar to the Tsaritsa, 1914–1917*, London 1929, p. 315.

7 'Tiazhelye dni. Sekretnye zasedaniia Soveta Ministrov 16 iul' – 2 sentiabr' 1915' [Difficult days. Secret meetings of the Council of Ministers, 16 July – 2 September 1915], *Arkhiv russkoi revoliutsii, [Archive of the Russian Revolution]* vol. 18, Berlin 1926, p. 15.

8 'Progressivnyi blok' [The Progressive Bloc], *Krasnyi Arkhiv [Red Archive]*, vol. 56, no. 1 (1933), p. 87.

9 Gosudarstvennaia Duma, *Stenograficheskie otchety [Stenographic reports]*, IV Duma, session V, col. 47, St Petersburg 1916.

10 *Rossiiskoe zakonodatel'stvo X–XX v. v 9 t.*, vol. 9, *Zakonodatel'stvo epokhi burzhuazno-demokraticheskhikh reform [Russian Legislation Xth – XXth Centuries in 9 Vols. Legislation of the Era of Bourgeois-Democratic Reforms]*, Moscow 1994, p. 122.

Further Reading

Billington, James H., *The Icon and the Axe: An Interpretive History of Russian Culture* (New York, 1966)

Dixon, Simon, *The Modernisation of Russia, 1676–1825* (Cambridge, 1999)

Hughes, Lindsey, *The Romanovs* (London, 2008)

Hughes, Lindsey, *Russia in the Age of Peter the Great* (London, 1998)

Kappeler, Andreas, *The Russian Empire* (Harlow, 2001)

Lieven, Dominic, *Nicholas II: Emperor of All the Russias* (London, 1993)

Moon, David, *The Russian Peasantry, 1600–1930* (London, 1999)

Raleigh, Donald J. (ed.), *The Emperors and Empresses of Russia: Rediscovering the Romanovs* (New York, 1996)

Waldron, Peter, *The End of Imperial Russia, 1855–1917* (London, 1997)

Wortman, Richard, *Scenarios of Power: Myth and Ceremony in Russian Monarchy* (Princeton, 2006)

Translations and Transcriptions of the Documents

1 Letter from Peter the Great to Ivan Tatishchev, governor of Novgorod, about the transport of horses for army regiments, 20 March 1710. Peter built up the Russian army and took a keen personal interest in the details of military matters. The previous year, he had defeated Charles XII of Sweden at the battle of Poltava.

> Mr commander
>
> When the horses from the Preobrazhenskii and Semenovskii regiments are sent to you from Koporii, check them against the lists and then stable and feed them either in Novgorod or in the countryside, whichever is more convenient.
>
> Peter
> From Petersburg, 20 March 1710

2 'A topographical depiction of the new Russian royal residence and harbour city of St Petersburg', printed in Nuremberg by Johannes Homann. The map is dated 1718. In the top right hand corner, Peter the Great is shown surrounded by the Muses and representations of the classical sciences. The map is as much a tribute to the Tsar as a depiction of the capital city he founded at the northwestern extremity of the empire.

3 Catherine the Great's charter to the nobility, 1785 (cover). The charter confirmed noble privileges, such as the right to petition Catherine directly and to attend provincial noble assemblies. These privileges were essential if the Russian state was to be able to continue to rely on the nobility to control the millions of serfs and maintain order in the countryside.

> By the grace of God, We Catherine II Empress and Autocrat of All the Russias, of Moscow, Kiev, Vladimir, Novgorod, Tsaritsa

of Kazan, Tsaritsa of Astrakhan, Tsaritsa of Siberia, Tsaritsa of Tauride Kherson, Sovereign of Pskov…

4 Letter from Grand Duke Alexander to Count Arakcheev, 31 August 1799. As heir to the throne during the reign of Paul I (1796–1801), Alexander was president of the War College and military governor of St Petersburg. Here he warns the de facto head of the army, Count Alexei Arakcheev, about two soldiers who will be placed under his command.

Mr General, Lieutenant of Artillery and Chief Inspector of Cavalry Arakcheev.

Information has reached me from the St Petersburg military commandant that you will be receiving Russian deserters from the Inspector of Infantry and the Finnish division, Golenishchev Kutuzov. Gunner Abdul Abliazov has arrived from abroad from the Swedish Vyborg artillery and Alexander Iakovlev, taken prisoner in the recent war with Sweden, was in service with the artillery there. In consideration of the danger of them serving in your regiment located in this region, I suggest for your consideration, General, that they be placed in troops in the rear or in a garrison.

Gatchina, 31 August 1799
Alexander

5 Card from a geographic set of the Russian empire. Produced in 1856, this card gave Russians some basic information about the Siberian province of Irkutsk. A map shows Irkutsk bordered by Enisei and Iakutsk provinces to the northwest and northeast respectively, and by China to the south. It is described as having a 'temperate climate' and an urban population of 19,975 people. The province's population is made up of 'Mungusy and Russians; the latter are here called Siberians'. The chief provincial centres are Irkutsk, Kirensk and Kiakhta and Irkutsk itself is 5,811 *verst* (5,446 km or 3,384 miles) from St Petersburg and 5,138 *verst* (4,828 km or 3,193 miles) from Moscow. The soil of the region is

described as 'loam and black earth' and the province's main industries are arable farming, hunting and trapping, fishing and pine nut oil extraction.

6 British petition to Tsar Nicholas II of May 1899. This petition was produced in support of Finland against the Russian empire's policy to limit Finland's autonomy, as part of its wider policy of 'Russification'.

London, May 1899

To His Imperial Majesty, the Tsar of all the Russias, Grand Duke of Finland, etc

May it please Your Majesty

We, the undersigned, venture respectfully to approach Your Majesty as profound sympathisers with the noble and enlightened sentiments to which Your Majesty has given expression in the Rescript which has resulted in the assembling of the Peace Conference, now in session at the Hague.

Having read and being deeply moved by the Petition of the 5th March (21st February) 1899 of over Half a million Finnish men & women in which they made a solemn appeal to Your Majesty in support of the maintenance of their full Rights and Privileges first confirmed by His Most Gracious and Imperial Majesty Alexander I, in 1809, both at the Diet of Borgo, and by the Treaty of Frederikshamn, and subsequently re-affirmed in the most solemn manner by all his Illustrious Successors, we venture to express our hope that Your Imperial Majesty will take into due consideration the prayer of the said petition of Your Majesty's Finnish Subjects.

It would be a matter of great regret to us, as to all admirers of Your Majesty's enlightened views if recent events in the Grand Duchy of Finland should retard the cause of amity among the

nations of the civilised world which has in Your Majesty so
Illustrious an Advocate.

Lister. President of the Royal Society
Clements. R. Markham. President of the Royal Geographical Society

7 Petition from the workmen of the Miuss tramway workshops in
Moscow, 13 January 1905, for better working conditions, transcribed in
1907 for a case in the Moscow district court. Their demands relate
entirely to their own environment, showing clearly the concerns that
occupied these workers early in 1905, when hundreds of thousands of
Russian workers came out on strike.

We ask for the following:

1   The easing of working conditions, by introducing an
    8-hour day in place of the existing 10-hour day.

2   An increase of 20% in our wages.

3   Evening and holiday working to be paid at 1½ times
    normal rates.

4   The workshops should have a medical attendant on
    permanent duty, with a doctor on duty at specified times.
    Medical advice should be free of charge both for the
    workers and for our families, i.e., our wives and children.

5   A pharmacy should be set up at the works and medicines
    should be made available free of charge.

6   The doctor and medical attendant should treat us with
    courtesy.

7   In cases of injury at work, and also during periods of
    illness, we should receive our wages as normal.

8   Forbid the foremen in the electrical workshop from
levying arbitary fines without the agreement of the
workshop manager.

The workers will not work until these matters have been
resolved.

8 Certificate from the Peasant Land Bank, 1912. The Peasant Land Bank
was established in 1883 by the Russian government to offer cheap loans
to the peasantry to enable them to buy land: it raised much of its capital
from foreign investors, especially in France. When the Bolsheviks seized
power in 1917, they repudiated all Russia's foreign debts, leaving
investors penniless.

IMPERIAL GOVERNMENT OF RUSSIA

Imperial 4½ % certificates OF THE PEASANT LAND BANK

second series of a nominal capital of 100.000.050 roubles =
266.666.800 francs

issued in conformity with the law of the 19 December 1911/1
January 1912 and the decision of the Committee of Finance,
sanctioned by H.M. the EMPEROR on the 17 February/1
March 1912.

CERTIFICATE

for a nominal capital of ONE HUNDRED AND FIFTY
ROUBLES (the rouble containing, in accordance with the
Monetary Law of 1899, 0,774234 gramme of fine gold) = 400
francs = 323 Reichsmarks 20 pf. = 15 pounds 17 shill. 7 1/5
pence sterl.

TO BEARER

The capital of these certificates is for ever exempt from any

Russian tax whatsoever. The interest is payable under deduction only of the tax of 5% on revenue derived from securities, which tax is at present in force in Russia; the interest is exempt, however, from any subsequent increase of the said tax and from the imposition of any other taxes, which may be levied in Russia. The regular payment of the interest and the repayment of the capital of these 4½ % certificates of the Peasant Land Bank are guaranteed as well by all real property mortgaged to the Peasant Land Bank and real property acquired for its own account, as by the entire resources of the State.

The certificates bear interest at the rate of 4½% per annum payable half-yearly, on the 1/14 March and 1/14 September in each year.

9 Propaganda postcard against Empress Alexandra, wife of Tsar Nicholas II. This postcard, which dates from early 1917, shows Empress Alexandra as a nurse (she and her daughters volunteered as nurses during the war). The banner at the top reads 'Alexandra', while the text around her reads 'German telegraph station'. The fly alludes to a derogatory nickname, 'the Hessian fly' – she was the daughter of the Grand Duke of Hesse, and the Hessian fly (*Mayetiola destructor*) was an agricultural pest known for damaging Russian crops. Many questioned the loyalty of the German-born Alexandra, and the suggestion here is that she was a German spy. The weeping crow is a parody of the German imperial eagle.

10 Report of 5 March 1917 in the *Herald of the Provisional Government* newspaper of the abdication of Tsar Nicholas II in favour of Grand Duke Michael, and Michael's refusal to accept the throne. Nicholas II did not want to abdicate in favour of his twelve-year-old son Aleksei, who suffered from haemophilia, and therefore passed the throne to his brother, Michael. But Michael had not been consulted and, after the leaders of the State Duma made it clear that his personal safety could not be guaranteed, he refused to accept the throne.

In these days of great struggle with an outside enemy, who has been trying for almost three years to enslave our native land, God has seen fit to visit a new and grievous trial on Russia. The internal disturbances which have begun among the people threaten to have a disastrous effect on the further conduct of a difficult war. The destiny of Russia, the honour of our heroic army, the welfare of our people, the entire future of our beloved Fatherland demand that the war be brought to a victorious conclusion no matter what the cost. The cruel foe is under great strain and it is already close to the time when our valiant army, together with our glorious allies, will be able finally to vanquish the enemy. In these decisive days for the life of Russia We have deemed it Our duty to assist Our people to draw closer together and to unite all Our people's forces for the rapid achievement of victory, and in agreement with the State Duma, We have recognised the benefit of abdicating from the Throne of the Russian State and to lay down Supreme power. Not wishing to be separated from Our beloved son, we pass Our inheritance to Our brother Grand Duke Michael Alexandrovich and bless Him on his accession to the Throne of the Russian State. We command Our brother to direct the affairs of the state in total and inviolable union with the representatives of the people in the legislative institutions on those foundations that will be established by them, and to take an inviolable oath to that effect. In the name of the dearly beloved native land, We call on all true sons of the Fatherland to carry out their sacred duty to It by obeying the Tsar at this difficult time of national trial and to help Him, together with the people's representatives, to lead the Russian State onto the path of victory, prosperity and glory. May the Lord God help Russia!

Nicholas
Pskov, 2 March, 3.05 pm, 1917

Abdication of Grand Duke Michael Alexandrovich

A heavy burden has been laid on Me by my brother who has passed to me the imperial throne of Russia at a time of unprecedented war and popular disturbances.

Animated by the thought which is in the minds of all, that the good of our native land is above other considerations, I have firmly decided to accept the supreme power only if that be the desire of our great people, expressed at a general election for their representatives to the Constituent Assembly, which should determine the form of government and lay down new fundamental laws for the Russian State.

Praying to God for His blessings, I beseech all citizens of the State to subject themselves to the Provisional Government, which is created by and invested with full power by the State Duma, until the summoning, at the earliest possible moment, of a Constituent Assembly, selected by universal, direct, equal, and secret ballot, which shall establish a government in accordance with the will of the people.

March 3, 1917
Petrograd

MICHAEL

Note on Dates and Names

Russia used the Julian calendar until February 1918; in the 19th century the Russian calendar was twelve days behind the West. Between 1900 and 1918 the difference was thirteen days.

Russian names have been transliterated to retain familiar spellings.

Sources of Illustrations

a = above, b = below, l = left, r = right

akg-images **6, 20, 27, 28, 46, 48, 54, 58, 60, 74, 94, 96, 98, 99, 103a, 107, 111, 115a, 116**; akg-images/British Library **39, 114**; akg-images/RIA Novosti **13, 18al, 24b, 32, 103b, 104–105, 118b**; akg-images/Sotheby's **18ar**; Arkhangelsk Museum/Bridgeman Art Library **33**; State Russian Museum, St Petersburg/Bridgeman Art Library **21**; Tretyakov Gallery, Moscow/Bridgeman Art Library **43**; Corbis **34, 35, 36a, 45, 49, 80b**; Mary Evans Picture Library/John Massey Stewart **78, 82**; Hamburgisches Museum für Völkerkunde, Hamburg **69b**; Illustrated London News **42a, 70, 71, 83, 84, 85**; iStockphoto.com **17, 97**; Russian State Archives of Film and Photographic documents, Krasnogorsk **75, 88, 91, 93, 121**; British Library, London **76**; British Museum, London **51**; State History Museum, Moscow **11, 125**; State Museums of the Moscow Kremlin **1, 15, 81, 120**; Tretyakov Gallery, Moscow **47, 52, 101, 102, 110**; Novgorod Cathedral **12**; Société de Géographie Française, Paris **42b**; Private Collection **31, 37, 38b, 56b, 68, 69a, 115b, 117a, 119, 126, 127, 128**; RIA Novosti **44, 109**; The Royal Collection Her Majesty Queen Elizabeth II **16**; Museum of Tsarskoye Selo, St Petersburg **55**; National Library of Russia, St Petersburg **63**; Pavlovsk Palace, St Petersburg **4–5, 56a**; Petrodvorets Palace, St Petersburg **53**; State Archive of Film & Photographic Documents, St Petersburg **112, 124**; State Hermitage Museum, St Petersburg **23, 29, 61, 65, 86, 87**; State Russian Museum, St Petersburg **8, 57, 106, 108, 113**; John Freeman for Thames & Hudson Ltd. **2–3, 14, 19, 24a, 38a, 59, 79, 123**; L. Tolstoy, *War and Peace*, 1930 **100**; E. Ukhtomsky, *Travels in the East of Nicholas II, Emperor of Russia*, 1896 **90b**; V&A Images, London **95**; David Warnes **11**; Library of Congress, Washington, D.C. **9, 30, 36b, 40–41, 62, 66, 67, 72, 77, 80a, 89, 90a**.

Facsimile documents

1 akg-images/RIA Novosti; **2** Harvard University Library, Cambridge; **3** Library of Congress, Washington, D.C.; **4** Daniel Bibb, danielbibb.com; **5** National Library of Russia, St Petersburg; **6** Bibliothèque Nordique, Paris/Archives Charmet/Bridgeman Art Library; **7** akg-images/RIA Novosti; **8** Private Collection; **9** Mary Evans Picture Library/John Massey Stewart; **10** Archives des Tsars, St Petersburg/Archives Charmet/Bridgeman Art Library.

Index

Page numbers in *italic* refer to illustrations